Bond

No.1 for exam success

Maths

Assessment Papers

Stretch

8-9 years

OXFORD
UNIVERSITY PRESS

OXFORD
UNIVERSITY PRESS

Great Clarendon Street, Oxford, OX2 6DP, United Kingdom

Oxford University Press is a department of the University of Oxford. It furthers the University's objective of excellence in research, scholarship, and education by publishing worldwide. Oxford is a registered trade mark of Oxford University Press in the UK and in certain other countries

First published in 2015

British Library Cataloguing in Publication Data
Data available

978-0-19-274209-4

10 9 8 7 6 5

Paper used in the production of this book is a natural, recyclable product made from wood grown in sustainable forests.
The manufacturing process conforms to the environmental regulations of the country of origin.

Printed in China

Acknowledgements

The publishers would like to thank the following for permissions to use copyright material:

Page make-up: GreenGate Publishing Services, Tonbridge, Kent
Cover illustrations: Lo Cole

Although we have made every effort to trace and contact all copyright holders before publication this has not been possible in all cases. If notified, the publisher will rectify any errors or omissions at the earliest opportunity.

Introduction

What is Bond?

The Bond *Stretch* titles are the most challenging of the Bond assessment papers, the number one series for the 11+, selective exams and general practice. Bond *Stretch* is carefully designed to challenge above and beyond the level provided in the regular Bond assessment range.

How does this book work?

The book contains two distinct sets of papers, along with full answers and a Progress Chart:

- Focus tests, accompanied by advice and directions, are focused on particular (and age-appropriate) Maths question types encountered in the 11+ and other exams, but devised at a higher level than the standard *Assessment Papers*. Each Focus test is designed to help raise a child's skills in the question type as well as offer plenty of practice for the necessary techniques.
- Mixed papers are full-length tests containing a full range of Maths question types. These are designed to provide rigorous practice for children working at a level higher than that required to pass at the 11+ and other Maths tests.

Full answers are provided for both types of test in the middle of the book.

Some questions may require a ruler or protractor. Calculators are not permitted.

How much time should the tests take?

The tests are for practice and to reinforce learning, and you may wish to test exam techniques and working to a set time limit. We would recommend your child spends 60 minutes to answer the 50 questions in each Mixed paper.

You can reduce the suggested time by five minutes to practise working at speed.

Using the Progress Chart

The Progress Chart can be used to track Focus test and Mixed paper results over time to monitor how well your child is doing and identify any repeated problems in tackling the different question types.

2mins left

Focus test 1 Place value

Circle the fraction that is the same as each decimal number.

> Remember: putting a zero on the end of a decimal doesn't change the number. 1.2 is the same as 1.20 and 1.200

1 0.8 → 8 $\frac{8}{10}$ $\frac{8}{100}$ $\frac{8}{1000}$

2 0.07 → 7 $\frac{7}{10}$ $\frac{7}{100}$ $\frac{7}{1000}$

3 Answer these.

$0.4 \times 10 =$ 40 $1.83 \times 10 =$ 8830 $19 \div 10 =$ 2.7 $2.7 \div 10 =$ ____

Write the number shown on each abacus.

4

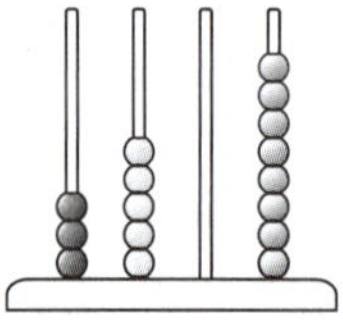

3508

5

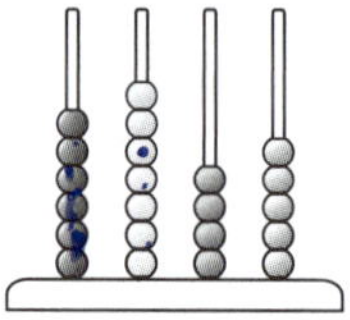

6745

6 Write the number that is at each position.

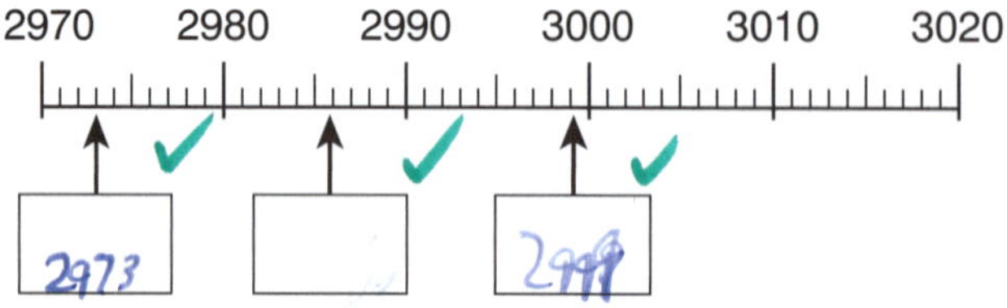

In each group of numbers, circle the smallest number and underline the largest number.

7 4621 4612 4162 4261 8 8400 8404 8044 8440

9 Write this set of decimals in order to make the number statement correct.

2.7 **7.02** **7.2** **2.72**

____ < ____ < ____ < ____

10 These are the lengths of four of the longest rivers in the world. Round each to the nearest 100 km.

River name	Amazon	Congo	Mississippi	Nile
Length	6387 km	4371 km	6270 km	6690 km
Round to nearest 100 km	6400	4400	6300	6700

Now go to the Progress Chart to record your score! Total 5 / 10

Focus test 2 Addition and subtraction

1 Complete these calculations.

```
  28.6        6503
  17.4      − 2879
+  9.2      ______
______
```

> Always estimate an approximate answer and then check your answer with the estimate at the end.

2 In Year 5 there are two classes. One has 29 pupils. The other has 32 pupils. On Wednesday there were 4 children away from each class.

How many children were there in the Year in total on Wednesday? ______

3 I'm thinking of a number. If I halve the number and then add 8 the answer is 30.

What number am I thinking of? ______

4 What is the difference between 28.5 and 35.2? ______

5 The cost of a holiday is £285 in April and £445 in July.

What is the difference in cost between the two months? ______

6 Write the missing digits, 1, 2 and 3, in this calculation.

```
    □ 8 □
+   4 4 9
_________
    6 □ 1
```

7 Add each row and column to find the figure in the bottom right-hand corner.

38	94	
72	43	

8 Join each pair of numbers that has a difference of 25.

47	53	38	37
62	63	72	28

9 What is the total weight of two boxes weighing 4.5 kg and 8.6 kg? ______

10 Jake has some 20p and 10p coins. He has three more 10p coins than 20p coins and altogether he has £1.50.

How many of each coin does he have?

______ 10p coins and ______ 20p coins

Now go to the Progress Chart to record your score! Total ___ 10

Focus test 3 Multiplication and division

1 Use each of the digits to complete the multiplications.

2 3 4 5 6 7

12 × 2 = 24 5 × 3 = 15 2 × 7 = 14

2 Write =, < or > to make each statement true.

57 ÷ 3 = 19 9 × 8 < 68 54 ÷ 6 < 12

3 This is a 'multiply by 6' machine. Write the missing numbers in the chart.

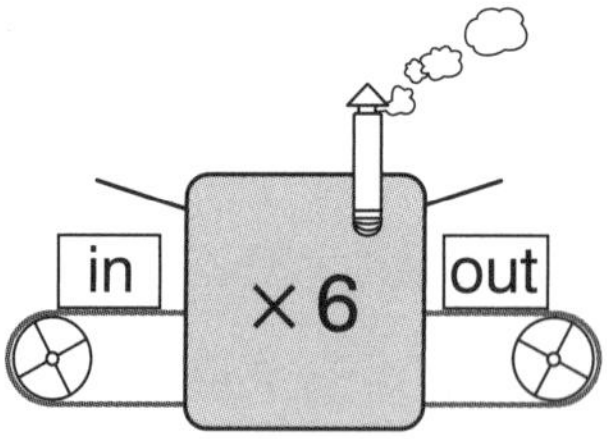

IN	7	3	9	6	4
OUT	42	18	54	36	24

? Sorrda noget

For this grid method multiply each pair of numbers to complete the grid. Then add up each row and find the total.

4 What is 56 multiplied by 28?

×	50	6	
20	1000	120	1120
8	400	48	448

Total: 1568

Example: What is 37 multiplied by 45?

×	30	7	
40	1200	280	1480
5	150	35	185

Total: 1665

5 Write in the missing number. 24 × 20 = 480

6 What is 1743 divided by 5? $\quad 5\overline{)1\,7\,4\,3}$ ______ r ___

7 A recipe makes 12 cakes each weighing 150 g.

What is the total weight of cakes made using this recipe? ______

8 David wants to buy a bike costing £92. He saves £8 a week.

How many weeks will he need to save before he can buy the bike?

______

9 Which number between 40 and 50 has a remainder of 2 when it is divided by 6? ______

10 Sam eats five cereal bars each week. There are eight bars in a pack.

How many packs are needed to last Sam for six weeks? ______

Now go to the Progress Chart to record your score! Total ◯ 10

Focus test 4 Multiples and factors

1 Circle the numbers that are multiples of 4.

24 30 56 80 62 54 84 75 63

2 Write each of these four numbers in the correct place on the Venn diagram.

21 32 25 30

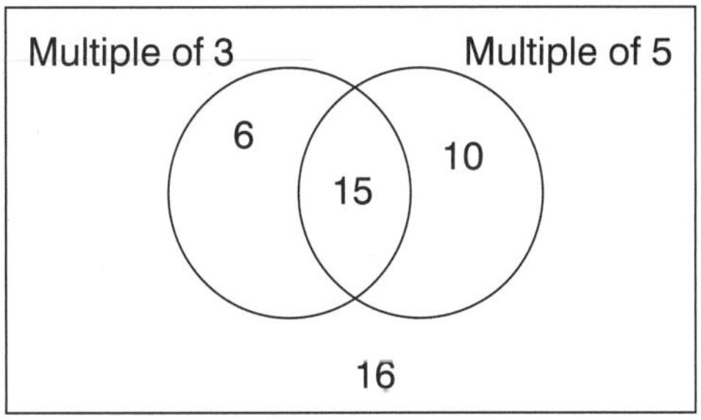

3 Ali says 'Only numbers ending in 5 are multiples of 5.'

Is he correct? Circle the answer: **yes** **no**

Explain how you know.

not errey mutiple of 5 ends in 5 e.g. 10 x 5 = 50

4 Write any multiple of 6 greater than 40. 42

5 What is the smallest number that is a multiple of both 4 and 10? 20

Factors are those numbers that will divide exactly into other numbers.
It is useful to put factors of numbers into pairs:

Factors of 15 → (1, 15) (3, 5) 15 has four factors.

6 Here are all the pairs of factors for a number.

Write the number and complete the first pair of factors.

24 → (1, 24) (2, 12) (3, 8) (4, 6)

7 Write the missing factors for 18.

18 → (1, 18) (2, 9) (3, 6)

8 Put a circle around the numbers that are factors of 21.

7 5 9 4 3 2 11

9 Prime numbers only have two factors. Write five different prime numbers that are less than 30.

(1,12) (2,8) (3,4) (5,3) (6,2)

10 Write all the pairs of factors for each of these numbers.

20	12
(1, 20)	(2, 6)
(5, 4)	(3, 4)
(2, 10)	(4, 3)

Now go to the Progress Chart to record your score! Total 10

Focus test 5 Fractions, decimals and percentages

1 What fraction of this shape is shaded?

Circle the answer.

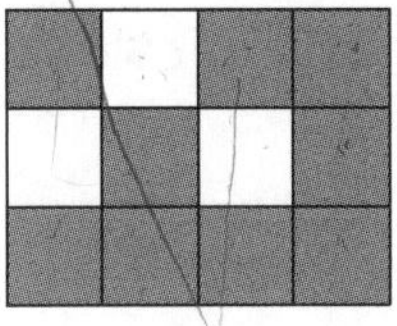

$\frac{1}{4}$ $\frac{1}{3}$ $\frac{2}{3}$ $\frac{3}{4}$

2 Put a tick in each row to complete this table.

	Greater than $\frac{1}{2}$	Less than $\frac{1}{2}$
0.35		✓
0.55	✓	
0.25		✓
0.05		✓

3 Complete these equivalent fraction chains.

$\frac{3}{4} = \frac{6}{8} = \frac{9}{12} = \frac{12}{16}$

$\frac{2}{3} = \frac{4}{6} = \frac{6}{9} = \frac{8}{12}$

4 Write < , > or = between each pair of fractions.

$\frac{2}{5}$ > $\frac{3}{10}$ $\frac{1}{2}$ = $\frac{3}{6}$ $\frac{6}{8}$ $\frac{3}{4}$ < $\frac{7}{8}$

5 Match each of these fraction calculations to its answer.

$\frac{1}{3}$ of 27

$\frac{1}{5}$ of 40

$\frac{1}{8}$ of 32

4
6
8
9
5
10

6 Write these fractions in order, starting with the smallest.

$\frac{8}{20}$ $\frac{2}{5}$ $\frac{7}{20}$ $\frac{10}{20}$ $\frac{1}{2}$ $\frac{3}{10}$ $\frac{6}{20}$ $\frac{3}{10}$ $\frac{7}{20}$ $\frac{2}{5}$ $\frac{1}{2}$

> Percentages are fractions out of 100. That's what per cent means: out of 100.
>
> % is the percentage sign.

7 What percentage of this pattern is shaded? 25%

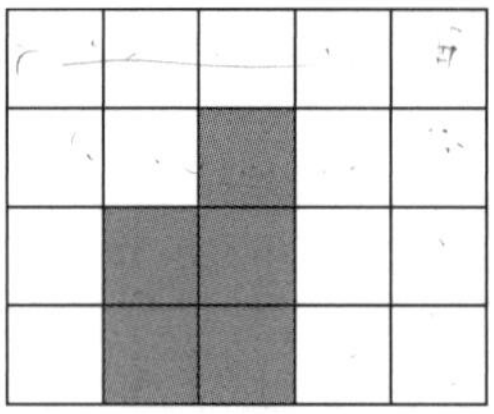

8 Write these fractions as percentages.

$\frac{3}{10}$ 30% $\frac{1}{2}$ 50% $\frac{1}{4}$ 25%

9 What is 75% as a fraction? Circle the answer.

$\frac{7}{50}$ $\frac{1}{4}$ $\frac{3}{4}$ $\frac{3}{25}$

10 Write these percentages as fractions.

10% $\frac{10}{100}$ 60% $\frac{60}{100}$ 80% $\frac{80}{100}$

Now go to the Progress Chart to record your score! Total ◯ 10

Focus test 6 Number sequences

If you need to find missing numbers in a sequence, look carefully at the numbers you are given. Try to work out the numbers next to these first, and then write the others.

1 What is the next number in this sequence?

67 64 61 58 55

2 What is the missing number in this sequence? Circle the answer.

9 16 25 36 49 64

38
36
32
40

Write the missing numbers in these sequences.

3 67 78 89 100 111 122

4 540 490 440 390 340 290

5 0.3 0.6 0.9 1.2 1.5 1.8

In these sequences each number is double the previous number.

Write the missing numbers.

6 1 2 4 8 16 32 64

7 25 50 100 200 400 800 1600

8 What is the next square number in this sequence?

25 36 49 64

5×5 6×6 7×7 8×8

Look at these number patterns. Write the next two numbers in each sequence.

9 9038 9036 9034 9032 9030 9028

10 2976 2981 2986 2991 2996 3001 3006

Now go to the Progress Chart to record your score! Total 10 / 10

Focus test 7 Shapes and angles

1 Write the letters for each shape in the correct position on the Carroll diagram.

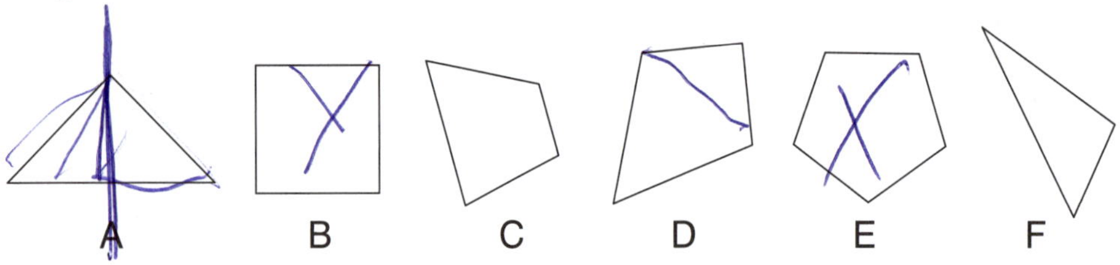

A B C D E F

	Symmetrical	Not symmetrical
Quadrilateral	B Square	C
Not a quadrilateral	E, A	F

2 Tick the right-angled triangle.

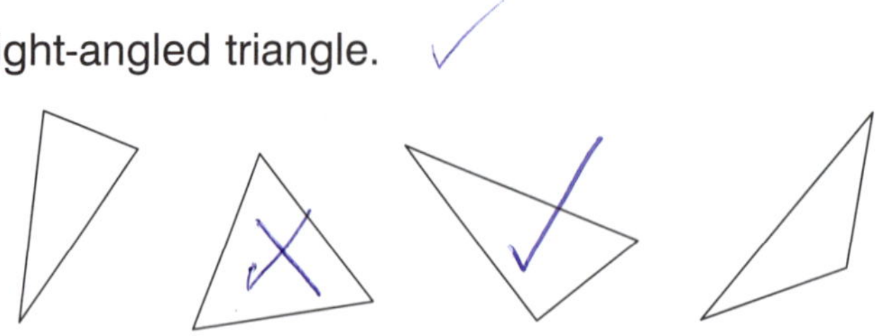

3 Sort these shapes into prisms and pyramids. Tick the correct box in the table for each shape.

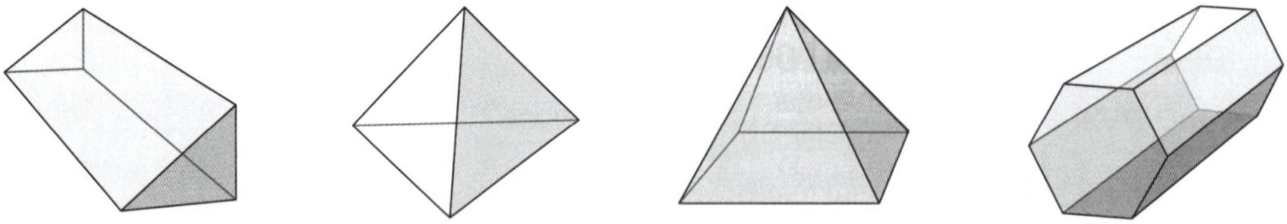

A B C D

	A	B	C	D
Pyramid		✓	✓	
Prism	✓			✓

4 Draw a quadrilateral on this grid.
It must only have one pair of parallel sides and two right angles.

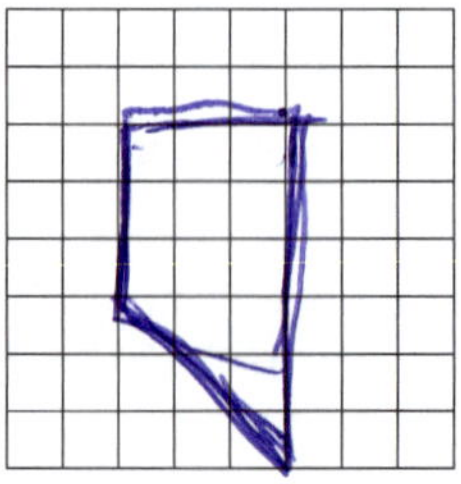

5 Tick the chart to show whether each angle is acute, obtuse or right-angled.

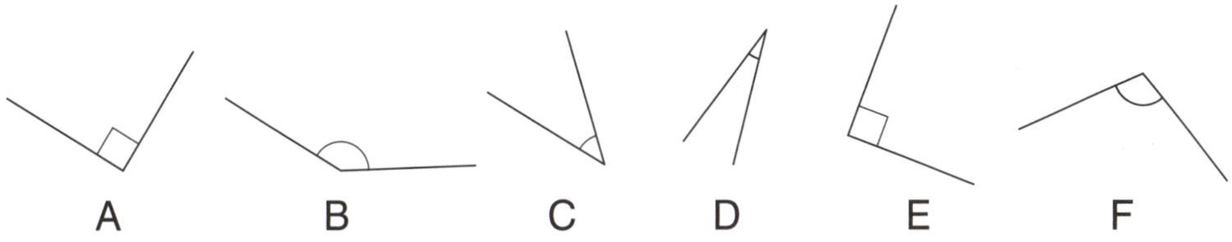

	A	B	C	D	E	F
Acute			✓	✗		
Obtuse		✓		✓		
Right-angled	✓				✓	F ✓

6 The dashed line is a mirror line. Shade more squares to show the reflection of the L-shape in the mirror line.

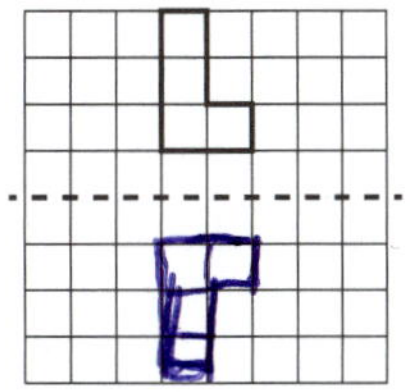

When a mirror is put on a line of symmetry the half shape and its reflection show the whole shape.

Write the name of each shape that is described.

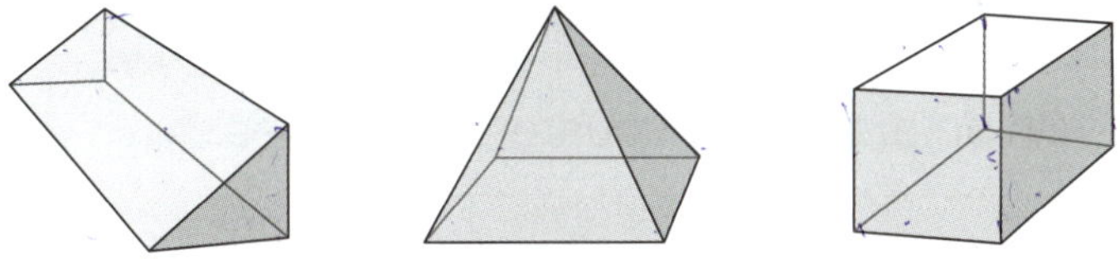

7 Which shape has 6 faces, 12 edges and 8 vertices? Sauer

8 Which shape has 5 faces, 8 edges and 5 vertices? prism

9 Which shape has 5 faces, 9 edges and 6 vertices? pyramid

10 Draw lines on this shape so that it would make a cube if you folded it. Use a ruler to measure where the lines go.

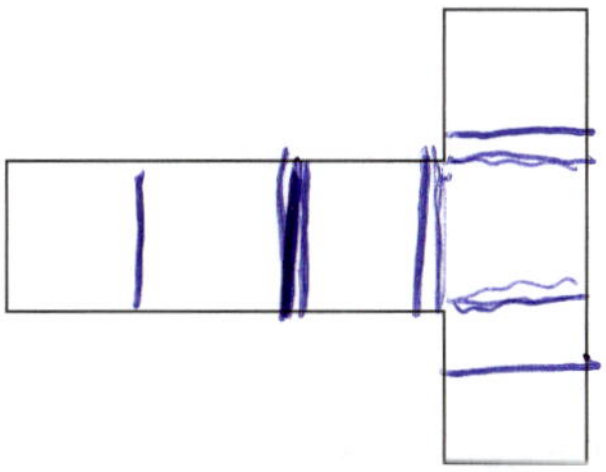

Now go to the Progress Chart to record your score! Total 6 / 10

Focus test 8 Area and perimeter

1 What is the approximate area of the shaded shape? Circle the correct answer.

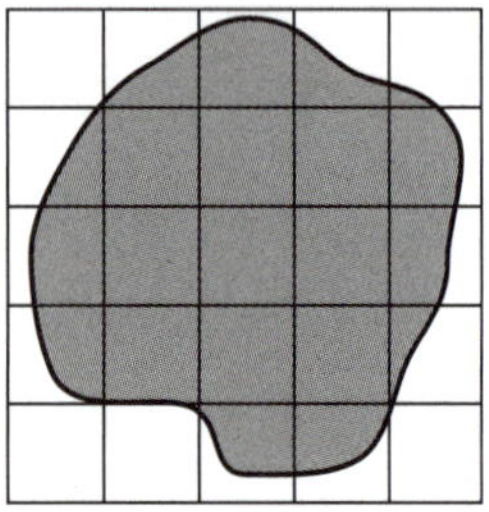

25 squares 15 squares (circled)

12 squares 20 squares

2 What are the area and perimeter of this rectangle?

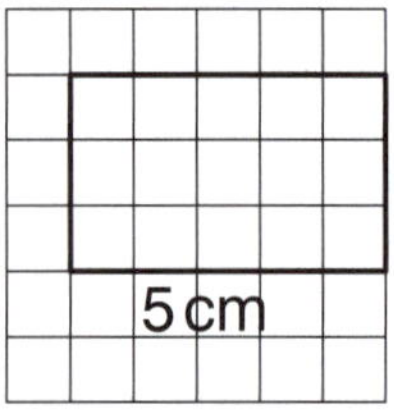

Area = 15 Cm

Perimeter = 16 Cm

> To find the area of a rectangle multiply the length by the width.
>
> Example:
>
> 
>
>
> Area = 3 cm × 4 cm = 12 square centimetres

3 Draw a rectangle with an area of 18 square centimetres.

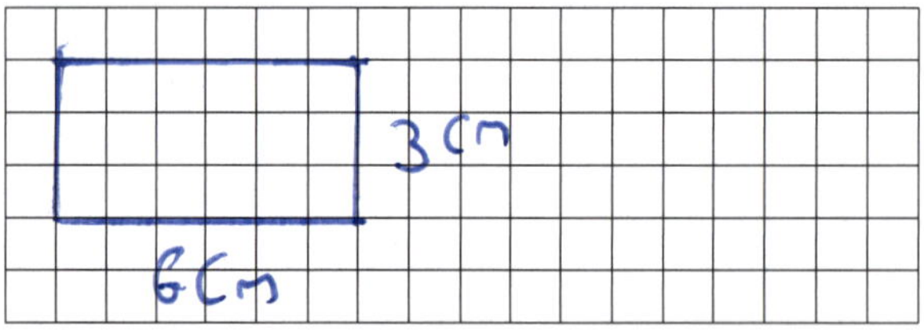

Calculate the area and perimeter of each of these rectangles.

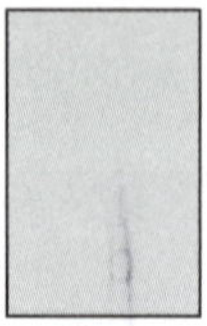

4 Area = 24 Cm

Perimeter = 22 Cm

5 Area = 35 Cm

Perimeter = 24 Cm

6 A rectangle has an area of 24 square centimetres and a perimeter of 20 cm.
Draw the rectangle on this square grid.

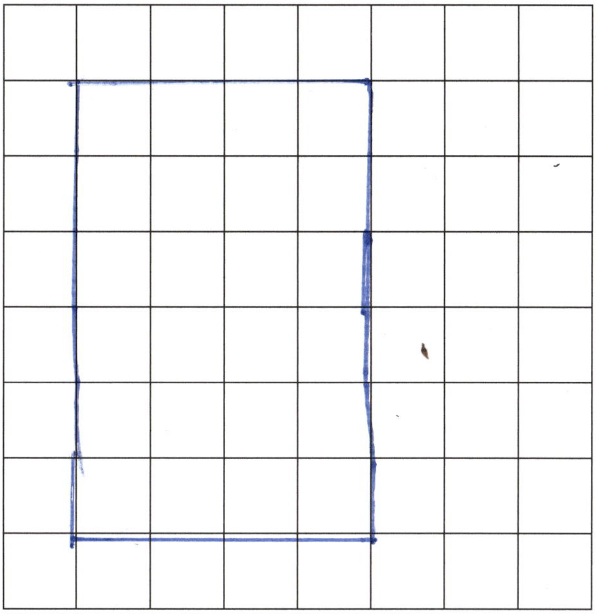

7 What is the perimeter of this shape?

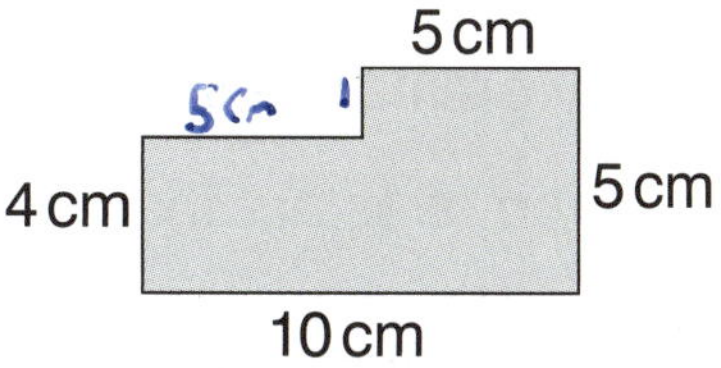

30 Cm

8 The area of this square is 16 square centimetres.

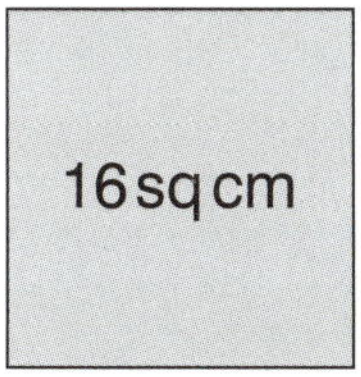

What is the length of each side?

4

9 What is the area of a square tile with a 12 cm side?

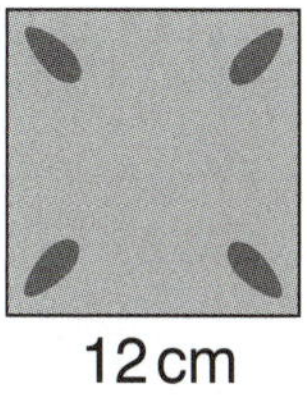

144 Cm

10 A farmer wants to put a length of electric wire round a field to keep in his sheep. The field is 50 m by 80 m.

What length electric wire will he need? 260 m

Now go to the Progress Chart to record your score! Total 10

Focus test 9 Measures

It is important to write the units in your answers, for example cm, ml or g.

1 Circle the correct measure for each of these items.

My drink bottle holds → 33 litres 30 ml 330 ml 3 ml

A plum weighs → 9 g 90 g 9 kg 90 kg

2 Write this set of measures in length order, starting with the smallest.

20 cm 220 mm 20 mm 2 m

____

3 Answer each of these questions.

How many millilitres are there in three litres? __________

How many grams are there in two and a half kilograms? __________

How many metres are there in one and a half kilometres? __________

4 Use a ruler to measure the length of side *a*.

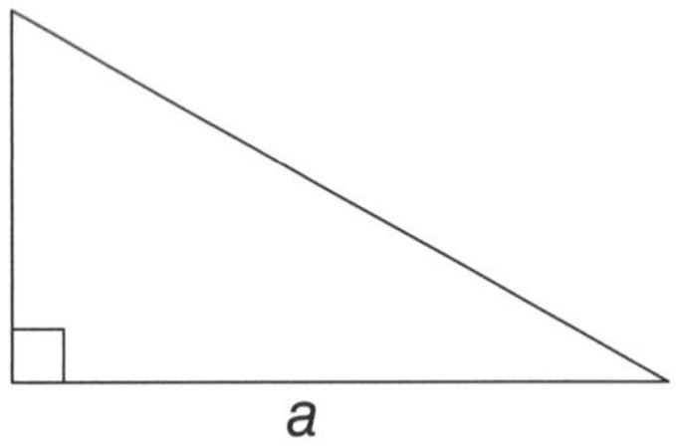

Give your answer in millimetres. __________

5 How much liquid is in this jug? __________

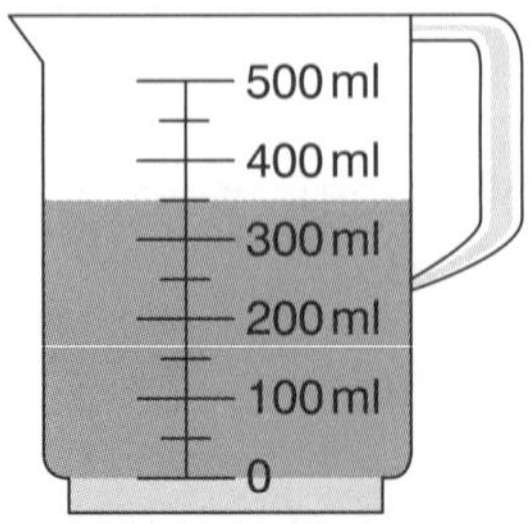

6 Draw an arrow on this scale to show 750 grams.

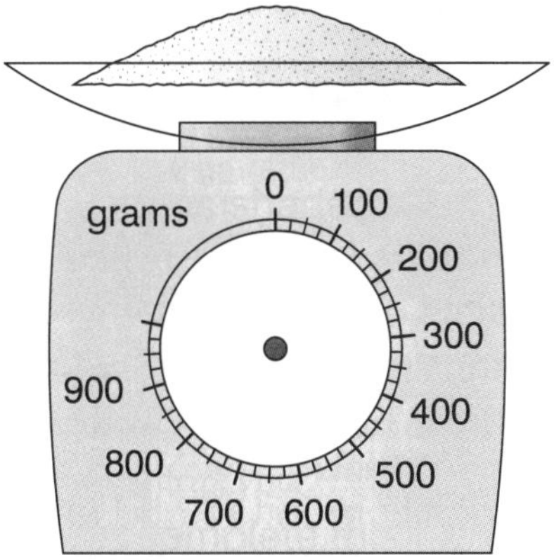

This clock shows the time when a TV programme ended.

7 At what time did the programme finish? ________

8 The programme lasted 55 minutes.

At what time did it start? ________

9 These shapes weigh 32 kg altogether.

If each cube weighs 4 kg, what is the weight of each sphere?

____

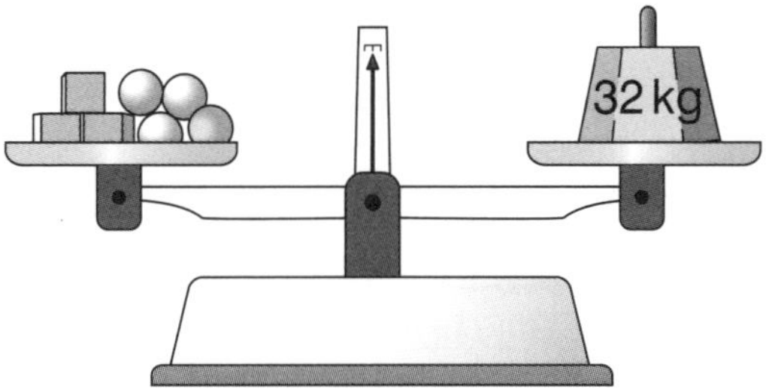

10 What is the difference in the amount of liquid in these two jugs?

____

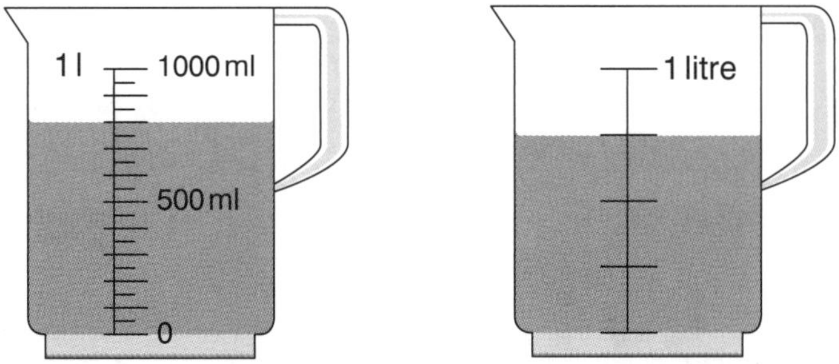

Now go to the Progress Chart to record your score! Total 10

Focus test 10 Position and movement

When you write coordinates, the number on the horizontal x-axis is written first, followed by the number on the vertical y-axis. You can remember this because x comes before y in the alphabet.

1–3 Plot each point in the correct position on the grid and label it with its letter.

A (4, 5)

B (0, 6)

C (2, 3)

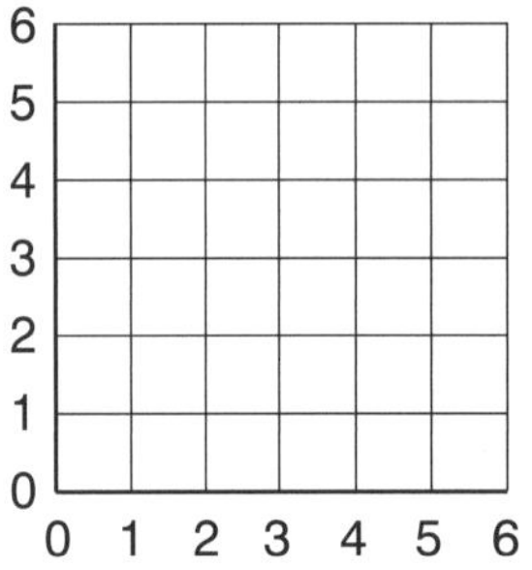

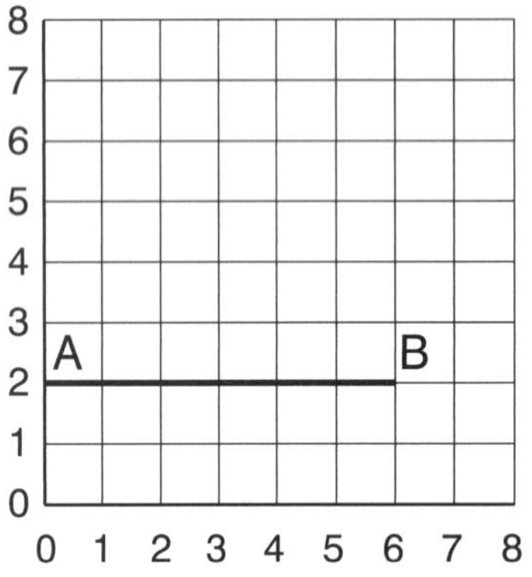

4 Circle the coordinates of point A. (2, 0) (0, 0) (0, 2) (6, 2)

5 Write the coordinates of point B. (_____ , _____)

6 Draw a cross at (7, 6) and label it C. Draw a cross at (1, 6) and label it D.

7 Join the points ABCD and then join D to A. What is the name of the shape you have drawn? ________________

8 Label the arrows pointing south, west and east with the letters S, W and E.

9 Label the arrows pointing SW, NE, NW and SE.

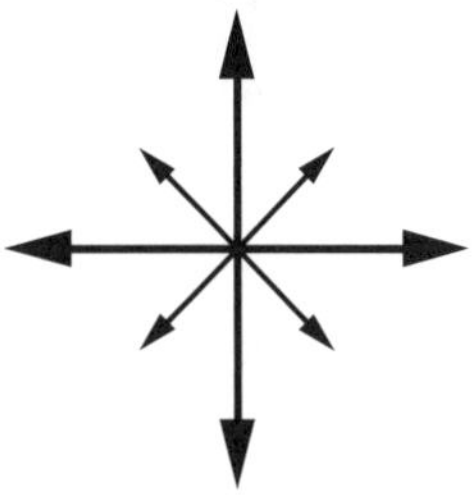

10 Complete this chart to show where you would be facing after each turn.

Start position, facing	Turn	End position, now facing
North	$\frac{1}{4}$ turn anticlockwise	________
South	$\frac{1}{2}$ turn clockwise	________
West	$\frac{1}{4}$ turn anticlockwise	________
East	$\frac{1}{4}$ turn clockwise	________

Now go to the Progress Chart to record your score! Total ◯ 10

Focus test 11 Charts, graphs and tables

This bar chart shows the number of ice creams sold on each day in one week.

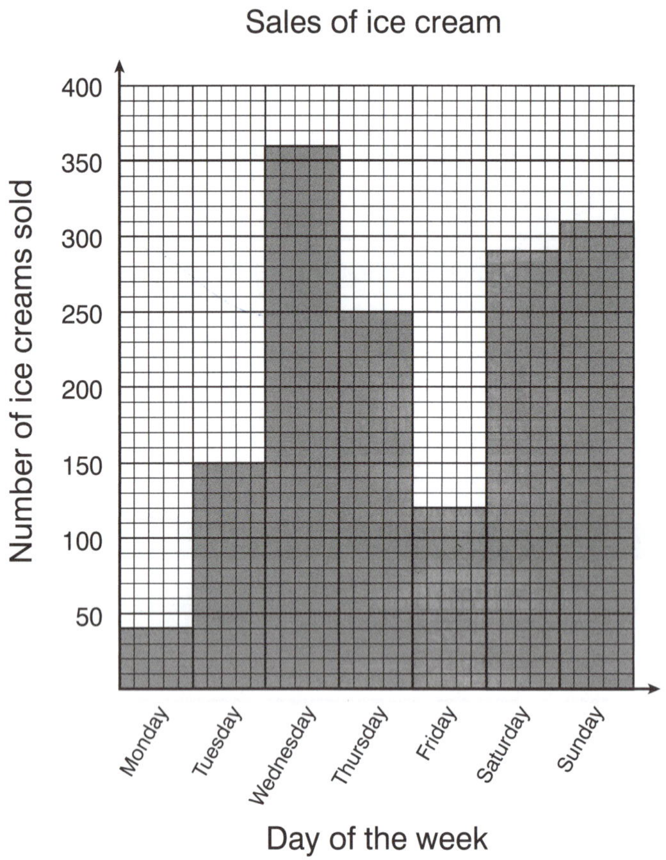

1 How many ice creams were sold on Friday? 120

2 On which day were 250 ice creams sold? Thursday

3 There was one very hot day. Which day do you think was very hot?

Wensday

4 How many more ice creams were sold on Sunday than Saturday?

20

5 How many ice creams were sold altogether on Monday and Tuesday?

190

This bar chart shows the number of books that were taken out from a school library and returned to the library each day of a week.

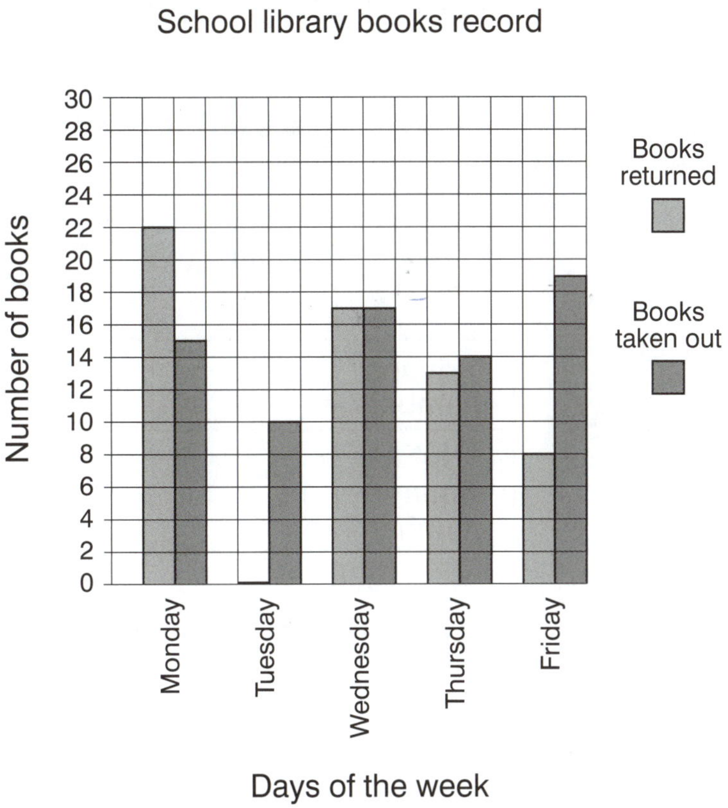

6 On which day were the most books taken out of the library?

Friday

7 On which day were no books brought back to the library?

Tuesday

8 How many more books were taken out than brought back on Friday?

11

9 On which day was the same number of books taken out and brought back? Wednesday

10 What was the total number of books taken out and brought back on Thursday? 27

Now go to the Progress Chart to record your score! Total 10 / 10

Focus test 12 Venn diagrams and Carroll diagrams

1–4 Write each of these numbers in the correct place on the Carroll diagram. Four numbers have been done for you.

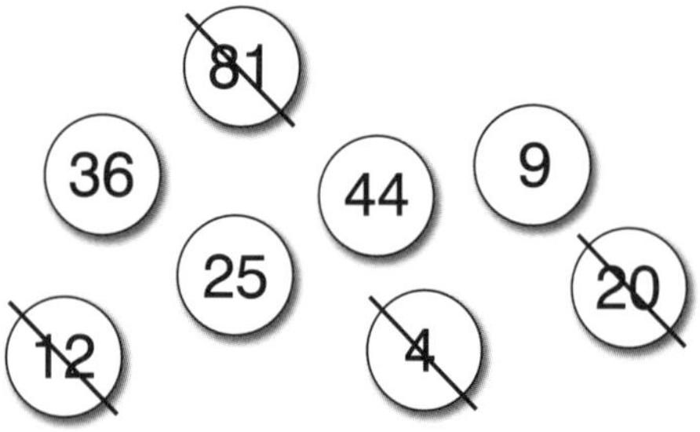

	Multiple of 3	Not a multiple of 3
Square number	81	4
Not a square number	12	20

5 Write each number from 1 to 15 in the correct place on the Venn diagram. Four numbers have been done for you.

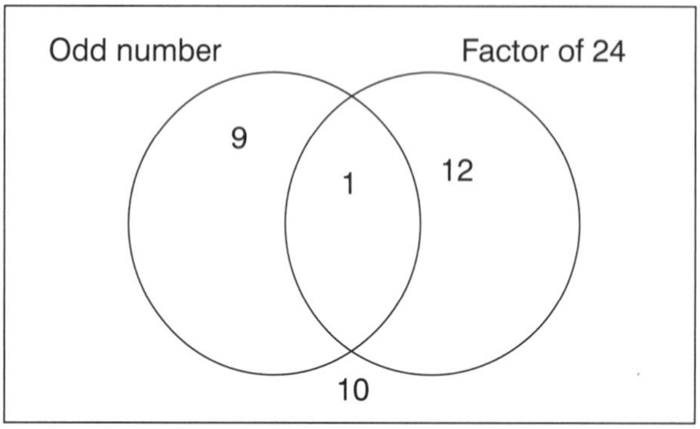

The top left section of a Carroll diagram matches the intersecting set of a Venn diagram that has the same information. The other sections of each diagram can also be matched.

	Odd number	Not an odd number
Factor of 24	1	12
Not a factor of 24	9	10

6–9 Draw each shape in the correct position on the Carroll diagram.

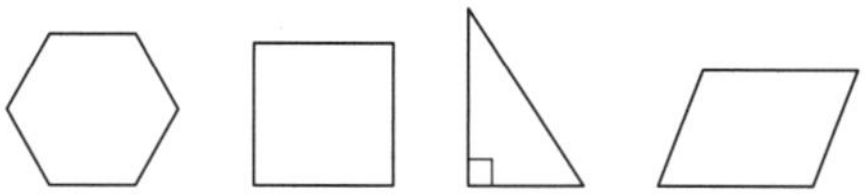

	Symmetrical	**Not symmetrical**
Has one or more right angles		
Has no right angles		

10 Write the letters for each shape in the correct position on the Venn diagram.

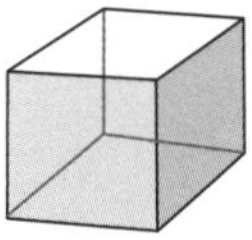

A

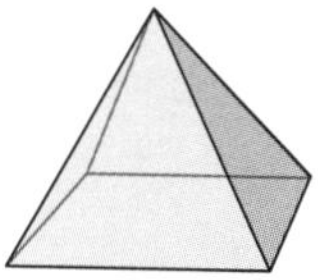

B

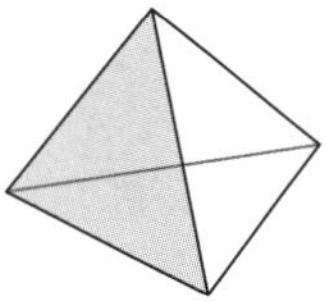

C

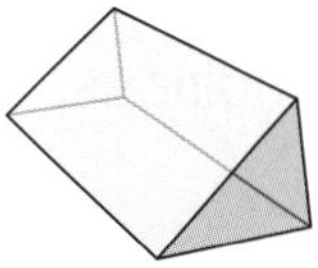

D

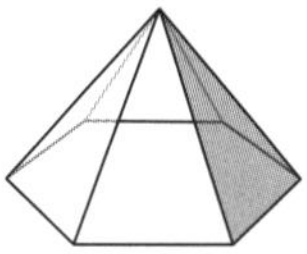

E

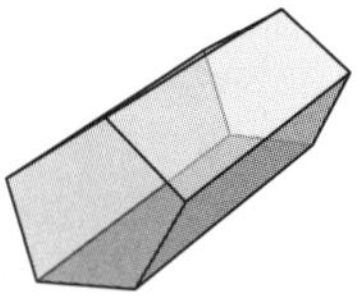

F

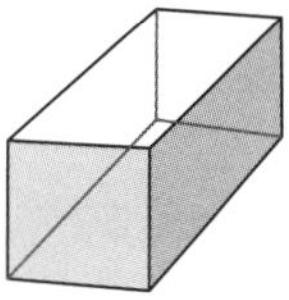

G

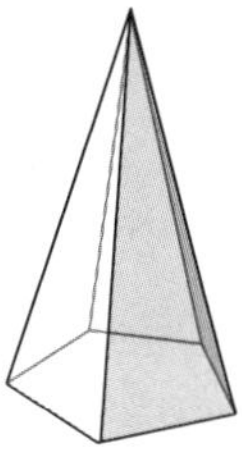

H

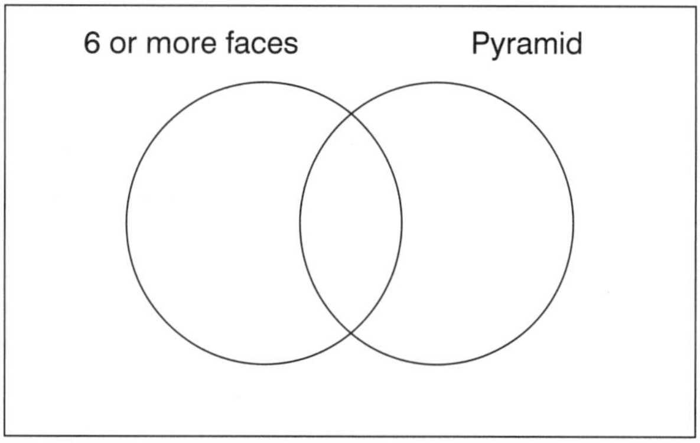

Now go to the Progress Chart to record your score! Total 10

Mixed paper 1

1–3 Write the number that is at each position on the number line.

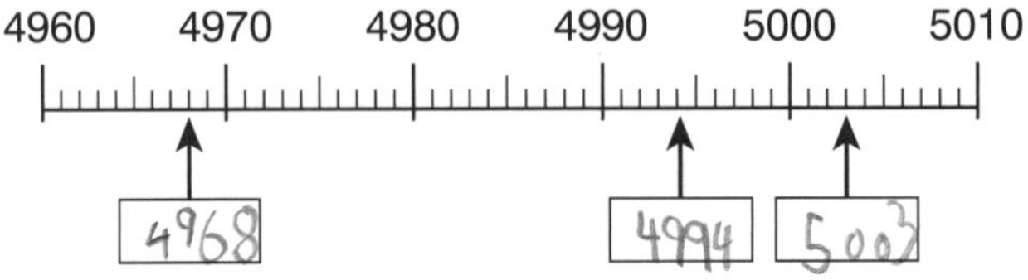

3

4 Write the number shown on the abacus. ________ 1

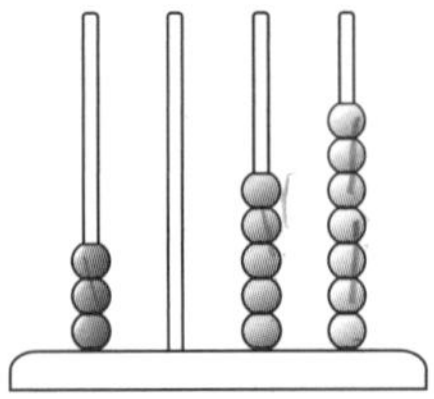

Complete these additions.

5

$$\begin{array}{r} 5869 \\ +\ 373 \\ \hline \end{array}$$

6

$$\begin{array}{r} 7704 \\ +\ 1698 \\ \hline \end{array}$$

2

7 What is 901 take away 552? ________

8 What is the difference between 178 and 4022? ________ 2

Write = , < or > to make each statement true.

9 3 × 6 ___ 5 × 4

10 6 × 4 ___ 8 × 3

11 15 ÷ 5 ___ 16 ÷ 4

12 30 ÷ 6 ___ 32 ÷ 8 4

13–14 Circle the two numbers that are a multiple of 3.

16 27 32 47 53 74 84 2

15–16 Write the missing pair of factors for 30.

30 → (1, 30) (2, 15) (3, 10) (___ , ___) 2

Look at the rectangle to answer these questions.

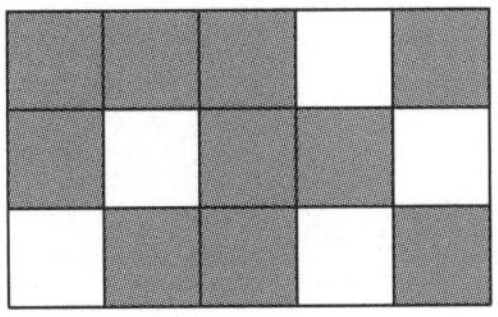

17 What fraction of this shape is shaded? Circle the answer.

$\frac{1}{2}$ $\frac{2}{3}$ $\frac{3}{4}$ $\frac{4}{5}$

18 Circle the fraction that is equivalent to the shaded part of this shape.

$\frac{15}{30}$ $\frac{20}{25}$ $\frac{30}{45}$ $\frac{15}{100}$ 2

19 What is $\frac{1}{5}$ of 15? ___

20 What is $\frac{1}{3}$ of 15? ___

21 Which fraction is smaller, $\frac{2}{5}$ or $\frac{1}{3}$? ___ 3

Write the next two numbers in each sequence.

22–23 52 55 58 61 _____ _____

24–25 4993 4983 4973 4963 _____ _____ 4

Answer these questions using the letters A to E.

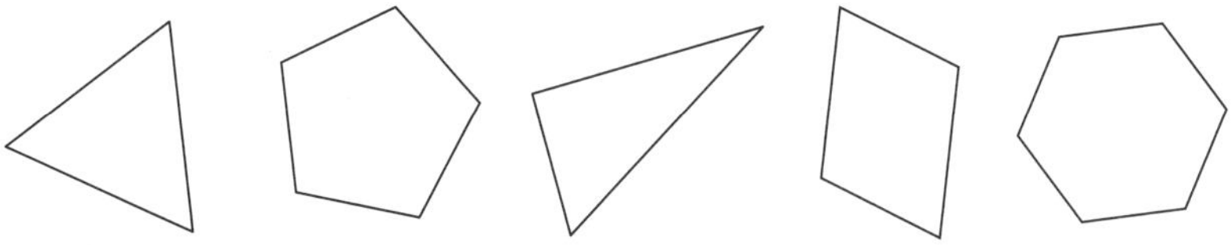

A B C D E

26 Which shape is a pentagon? _____

27 Which shape has a right angle? _____

28 Which shape has exactly three lines of symmetry? _____

29 Which two shapes have parallel sides? _____ and _____ 4

30 How many lines of symmetry do squares have? _____ 1

What are the area and perimeter of each of these rectangles?

31–32

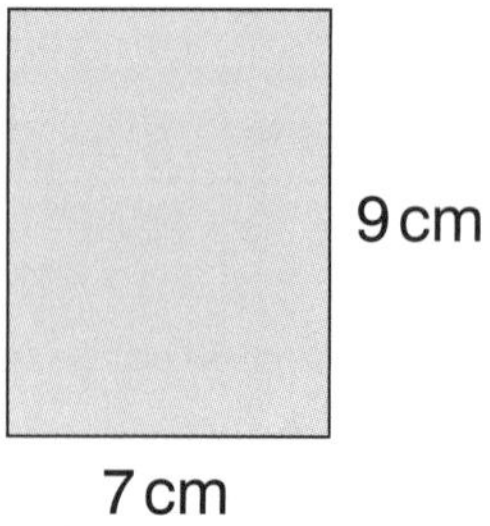

Area = ______________

Perimeter = ______________

33–34

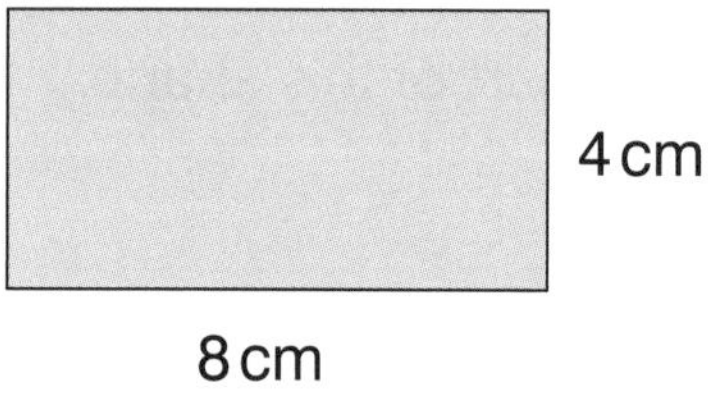

Area = ______________

Perimeter = ______________

4

35–38 Write these measures in order, starting with the smallest.

1 m   107 cm   71 mm   7 cm   _____ _____ _____ _____

smallest

4

39 Circle the coordinates of point A.

(0, 3)   (5, 0)   (3, 5)   (5, 3)   (3, 3)

40 What are the coordinates of point B?

(_____ , _____)

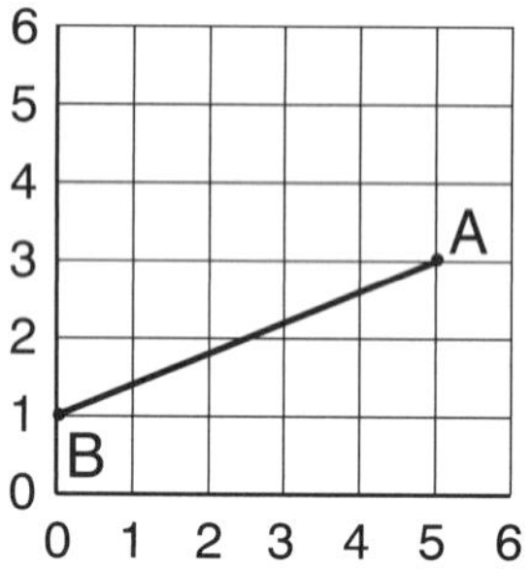

2

This pictogram shows the results of a survey on favourite pizza toppings.

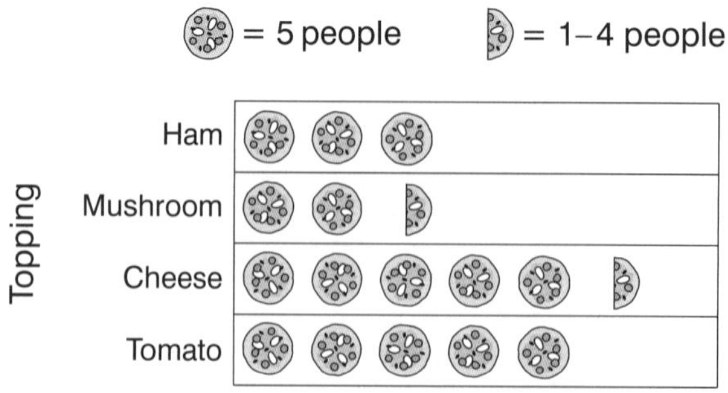

Favourite pizza toppings

41 How many people chose ham as their favourite pizza topping? _____

42 Which topping did 26–29 people choose as their favourite pizza topping? _____

43 How many more people preferred tomato to ham? _____

44 Circle the most likely number of people who chose mushroom as their favourite topping.

25 $2\frac{1}{2}$ 15 12

4

This Carroll diagram shows the shoes worn by a group of children.

Shoes	Laces	No laces
Black	Ali, Eve	Jack, Harry
Brown	Cara, Aidan, Haley, Ava, Emma	Beth

45 How many children are wearing shoes with laces? _____

46 How many children are wearing black shoes with laces? _____

47 Who is wearing brown shoes with no laces? __________

48 How many children are not wearing black shoes? _____

4

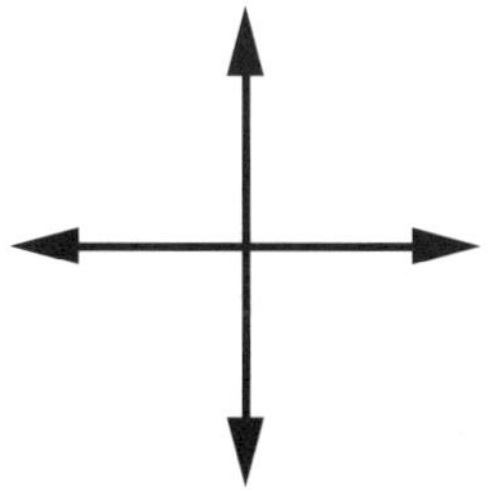

49 Label the arrow pointing north with an N.

50 If I faced north and made a half-turn clockwise, which direction would I be facing? Circle the answer.

north west south east

2

Now go to the Progress Chart to record your score! Total 50

Mixed paper 2

In each group of numbers, circle the smallest number and underline the largest number.

1–2 2793 3297 2379 3729

3–4 6110 6001 6011 6101 4

A bakery has a café. These are the number of sandwiches and cakes that are bought to eat in or eat out in one week.

	Eat in	Eat out
Sandwiches	740	1319
Cakes	2808	1956

5 How many cakes and sandwiches in total were sold to eat in? 3548

6 How many cakes and sandwiches in total were sold to eat out? 3275

7 How many more sandwiches were sold to eat out than eat in? 579

8 How many more cakes were sold to eat in than eat out? 852

9 How many more cakes than sandwiches were sold in total? _____ 5

10–13 This is a 'multiply by 7' machine. Write the missing numbers in the chart.

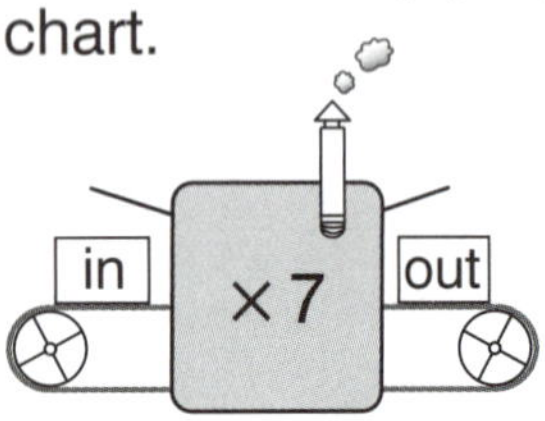

IN	4	6	9	20	50
OUT	28	42	63	140	350

4

Choose from these numbers to answer each question.

5 15 9 12 6 18

14 Which number is a multiple of 4? 12

15 Which number is a prime number? 5

16 Which number is a factor of 70? 15

17 Which number is a factor of 63? 9

18 Which number is a square number? 9 5

Write these decimals as whole numbers and fractions.

19 2.7 → $2\frac{7}{10}$ **20** 4.2 → $4\frac{2}{10}$ 2

Write < or > to make these statements true.

21 8.5 > $8\frac{1}{5}$ **22** $4\frac{3}{10}$ > $3\frac{4}{10}$ 2

23 What is the missing number in this sequence?

6.2 6.7 7.2 7.7 8.2

24 What is the first number in this sequence?

2404 2409 2414 2419 2424

25–26 Write the missing numbers in this sequence.

95 87 79 71 63 55 4

27 Circle the cube.

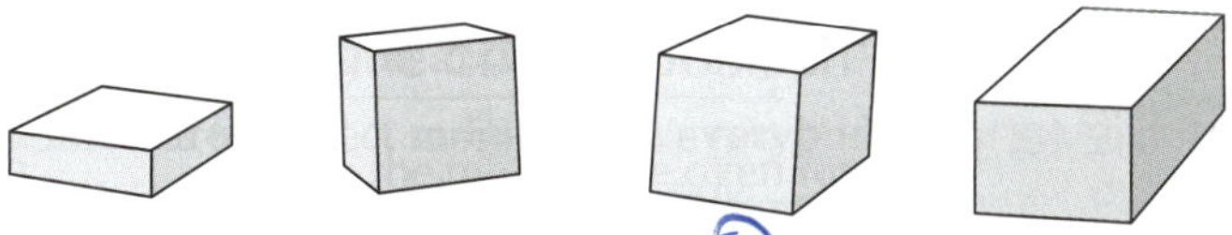

A B (C) D

28 Draw a circle around each shape that is symmetrical.

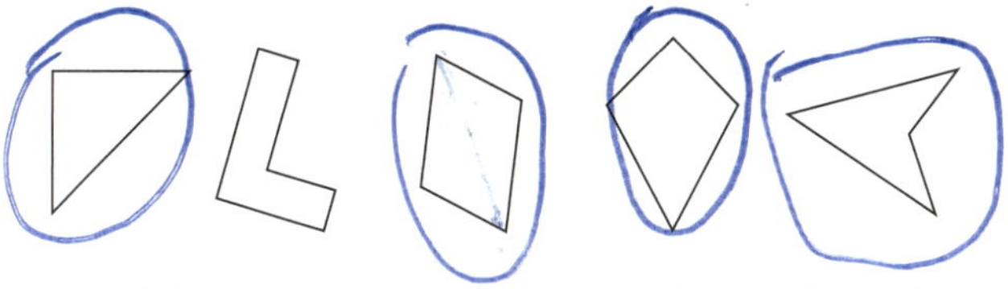

2

29 Look at this pentagon and write the letter of the correct angle to complete this statement.

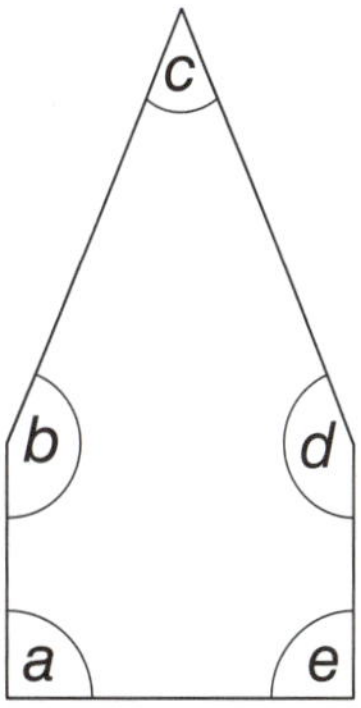

Angle ____ is an acute angle. 1

30 Draw a circle around each of the pyramids.

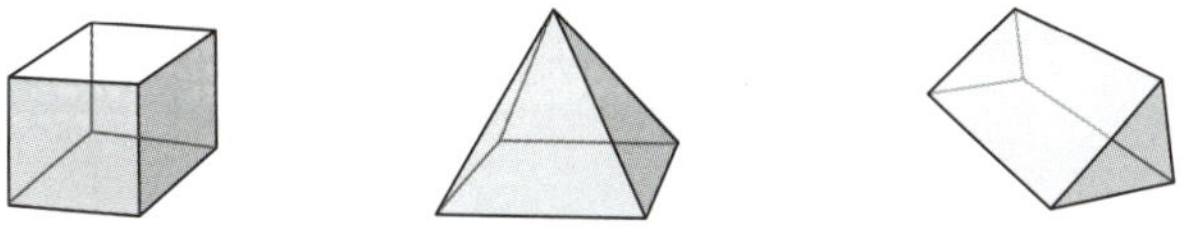

A B C

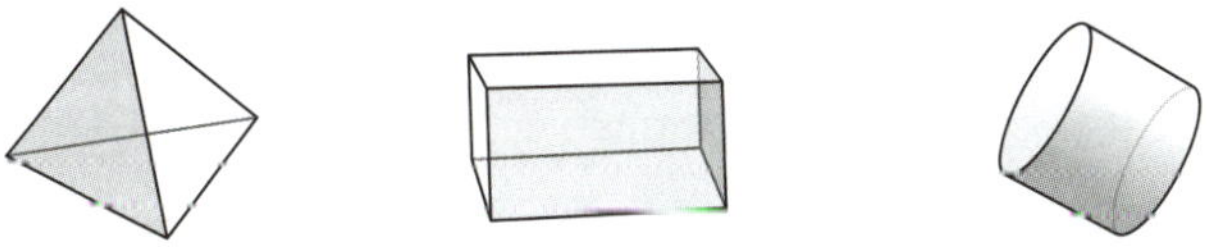

D E F 1

Look at these shapes and answer the questions.

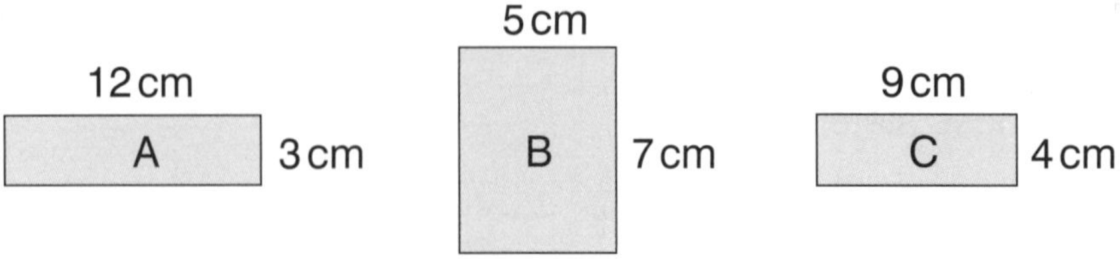

31 Write the letter of the rectangle that does **not** have an area of 36 square centimetres. _____

32 Write the letter of the rectangle that has a perimeter of 26cm. _____ 2

33 A rectangular field has two sides each 350m long. The other two sides are 125m in length.

What is the total length of fencing that is needed to go around this field? _______ 1

34 A square has an area of 81 square centimetres.

What is the length of its perimeter?

18cm 9cm 36cm 49cm 1

Circle the correct measure for each of these items.

35 A birthday card weighs → 10g 500g 1kg 10kg

36 A full bucket holds → 10ml 500ml 1 litre 10 litres 2

37 How many centimetres are there in 4 metres? _____cm

38 How many metres are there in 3 kilometres? _____m 2

39 Label the arrow pointing east with an E.

40 Label the arrow pointing west with a W. 2

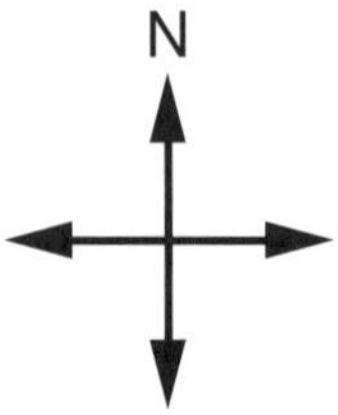

Plot each point in the correct position on the grid and label it with its letter.

41 A (4, 2)

42 B (0, 3) 2

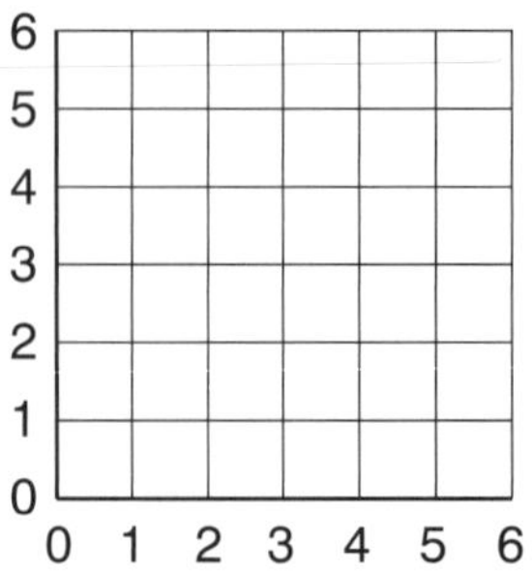

This graph shows the points scored by players on a Treasure Hunt game app.

43 How many points did Lily score? ____

44 Who scored 49 points? ________

45 What is the points difference between the player with the most points and the player with the fewest points? ____

46 Who scored four more points than Noel? ________

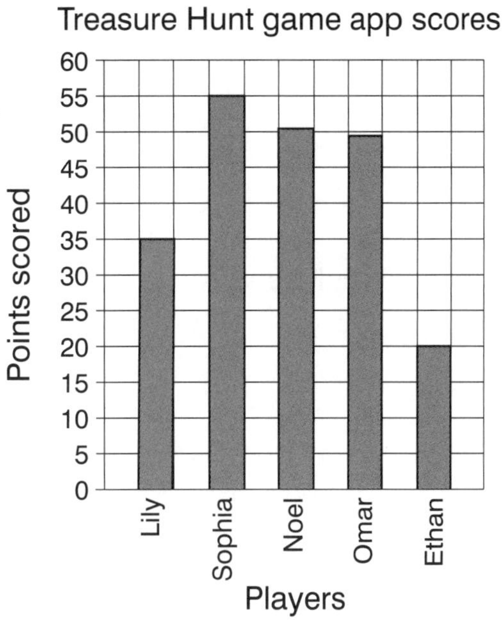

4

The first six months of the year have been sorted on this Venn diagram.

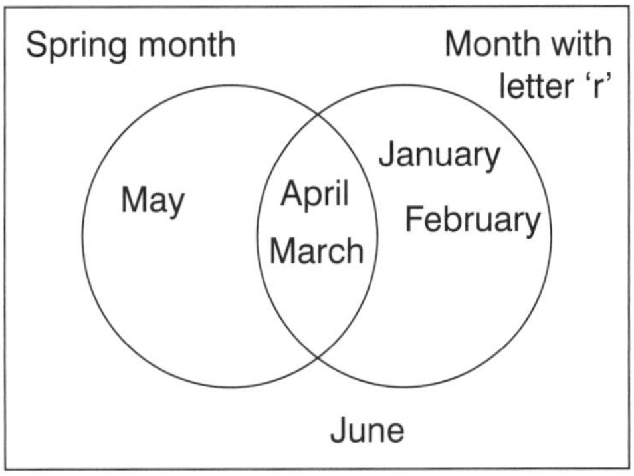

47 How many months have the letter 'r' and are in the spring? ________

48 Which month is in the spring but does not have the letter 'r' in it?

____

49 How many months in the first half of the year have the letter 'r' in them? ________

50 Write **August** in the correct section on the Venn diagram.

4

Now go to the Progress Chart to record your score! **Total** 50

Mixed paper 3

Circle the fraction that is the same as each decimal number.

1 0.3   3 $\frac{3}{10}$ $\frac{3}{100}$ $\frac{3}{1000}$

2 0.09   9 $\frac{9}{10}$ $\frac{9}{100}$ $\frac{9}{1000}$ 2

Complete these calculations.

3 1.52 × 10 = _____

4 34 ÷ 10 = _____   2

5 Lee is 162 cm tall and his younger sister Mia is 139 cm tall. How much taller is Lee than his sister Mia? ________

6 A shopping basket has a 2.55 kg bag of potatoes, a 1.75 kg box of washing powder and a 1.2 kg bag of onions. What is the total weight of shopping in this basket? ________   2

Look at these two numbers and answer the questions.

7493	1660

7 What is the difference between these two numbers? _____   2

8 What is the total when these two numbers are added together? _____   2

9 Three pizzas weigh 285 g. What is the weight of one pizza? ________

10 Individual pizzas cost 89p each. This 3-pack special offer is 50p cheaper than buying three individual pizzas. How much does the 3-pack special offer cost? ________   2

Write the missing numbers.

11 13 × ___ = 260

12 180 ÷ ___ = 6

13 12 × ___ = 600   3

14–17 Write each of these numbers in the correct part of the Carroll diagram.

2	8	12	18

	A factor of 16	Not a factor of 16
A multiple of 4	______	______
Not a multiple of 4	______	______

4

Write < , > or = between each pair.

18 $\frac{1}{2}$ __ 0.25 **19** $\frac{2}{5}$ __ $\frac{5}{10}$

20 $\frac{1}{3}$ of 12 __ $\frac{1}{2}$ of 8 **21** 40% __ $\frac{4}{10}$ 4

Write the missing numbers in these sequences.

22–23 ____ 553 523 493 ____

24–25 ____ 12 24 48 ____ 4

26 Which of one these nets can be folded to make a cube?
Circle the correct letter.

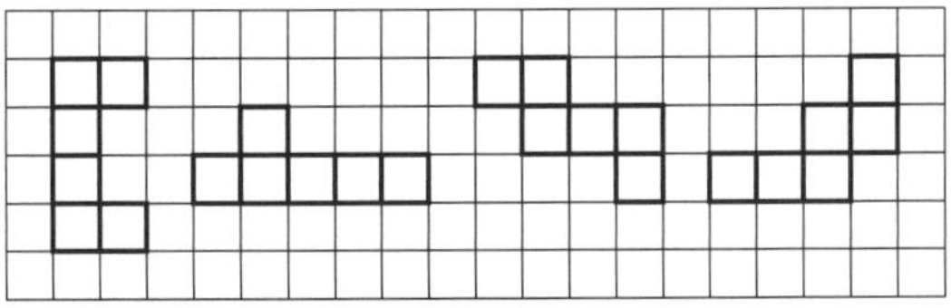

A B C D 1

27 Write the name of this shape. ____________ 1

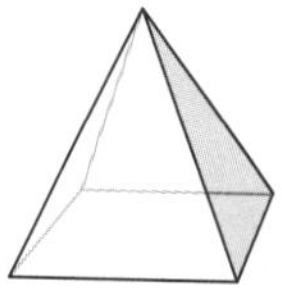

Look at this triangle.

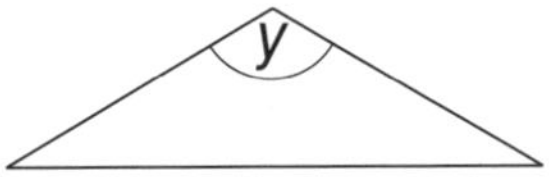

28 What is the name of this triangle? Underline the answer.

equilateral isosceles right-angled scalene

29 What type of angle is angle *y*? Underline the answer.

right angle acute obtuse 2

30 The area of a square is 36 square metres.

What is the length of each side? _____ 1

Draw two rectangles, each with an area of 12 square centimetres and these perimeters.

31 Perimeter = 16 cm

32 Perimeter = 14 cm

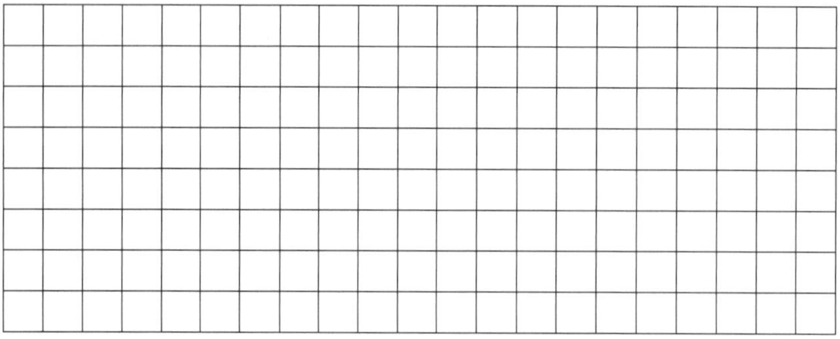

2

33 What is the area of this shape? Circle the answer.

8 squares

12 squares

14 squares

16 squares

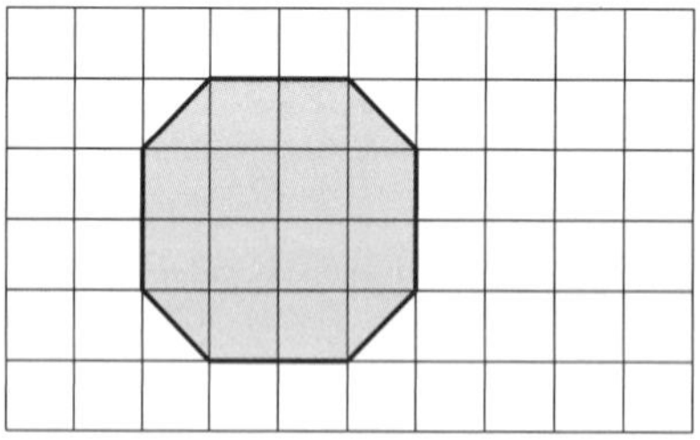

1

34–35 How much water is there in each jug?

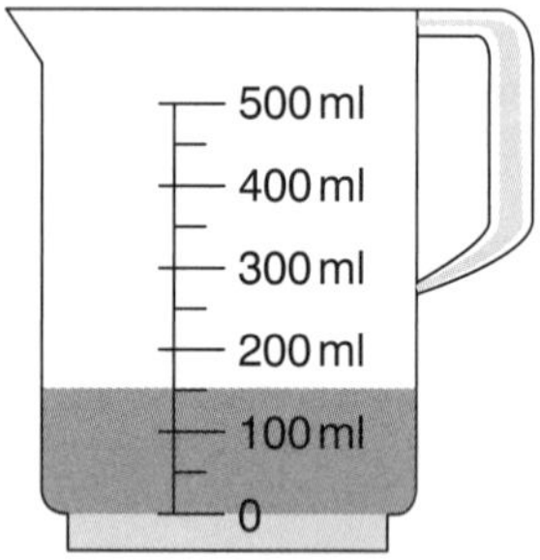

_________ ml

_________ ml

36 What is the difference in the amount of water between these two jugs?

____

37 If the water from these two jugs were poured into one bottle, how much water would there be in total in the bottle? _________ 4

38 Draw a cross at (6, 3) and label it C.

39 Write the coordinates for point A.

(_____ , _____)

40 Circle the coordinates for point B.

(5, 4) (5, 1) (4, 5) (1, 5)

41 Join points ABC and then join C to A.

What shape have you drawn?

____

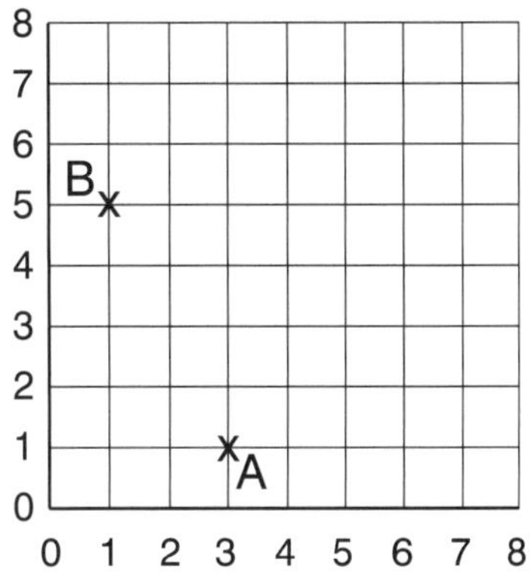

4

This graph shows the number of each type of pet that a vet saw in one month.

Animals visiting a vet

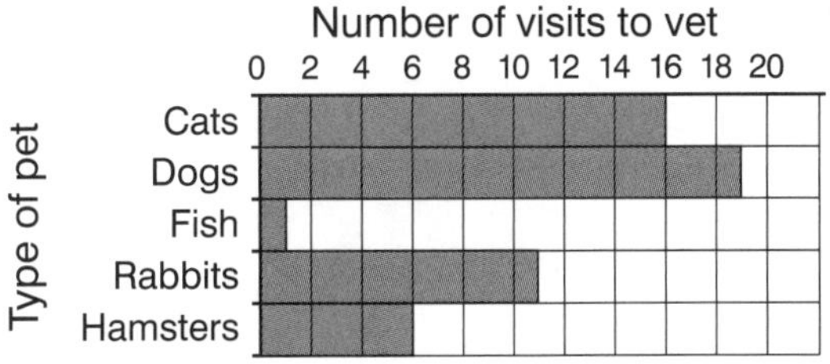

42 Which type of pet did the vet see the most? __________

43 Which type of pet did the vet see only one of? __________

44 How many more dogs than cats did the vet see? __________

45 How many hamsters and rabbits did the vet see in total? __________

4

46–49 Write the circled numbers in the correct place on the Carroll diagram.

~~1~~ ~~2~~ ~~3~~ ~~4~~ ~~5~~ ~~6~~ ~~7~~ ~~8~~ ~~9~~ ~~10~~ (11) ~~12~~ ~~13~~ (14) ~~15~~ ~~16~~ ~~17~~ ~~18~~ ~~19~~ ~~20~~ (21) ~~22~~ ~~23~~ (24) ~~25~~ ~~26~~ ~~27~~ ~~28~~ ~~29~~ ~~30~~

	Even number	**Not an even number**
Multiple of 7	28	7
Not a multiple of 7	16 2 26 4 18 6 20 8 10 12 22 30	23 15 1 3 17 27 19 5 13 29 9 25

4

50 How many even numbers between 1 and 30 are not multiples of 7?

____

1

Now go to the Progress Chart to record your score! Total 50

Mixed paper 4

1–4 Write this set of decimals in order to make the number statement correct.

5.08	80.5	8.5	5.85

_____ < _____ < _____ < _____ 4

Look at these decimal numbers.

29.7	52.3	64.9	13.5

5 What is the difference between the largest number and the smallest number? _____

6 What is the largest total that can be made from adding two of these numbers? _____

7 What is the smallest total that can be made from adding two of these numbers? _____

8 What is the smallest difference that can be made between two numbers? _____ 4

There are 3 classes each with 30 children going on a school trip with 12 adults.

9 The children are divided equally between 2 buses and there will be 6 adults on each bus. The buses will have all their seats full.

How many seats are there on each bus? _____

10 The children are put into equal-sized groups with 2 adults looking after each group.

How many adults and children in total will there be in each group?

_____

Choose **one** of these methods to calculate the answer.

11 $342 \times 6 =$ _________

×	300	40	2
6			

→ _____

$$\begin{array}{r} 342 \\ \times \quad 6 \\ \hline \\ \hline \end{array}$$

1

12 Complete this division. $4\overline{)953}$

(1)

Are these statements 'true' or 'false'? Circle the answer for each.

13 A multiple of 3 is always an odd number. **true** **false**

14 A multiple of 4 is always an even number. **true** **false**

(2)

15 Write a number between 15 and 20 that is a factor of 36.

15 < ____ < 20

(1)

16 Here are all the pairs of factors for a number.

Write the number and complete the first pair of factors.

____ → (1, ____) (2, 30) (3, 20) (4, 15) (5, 12) (6, 10)

(1)

17–20 Write these fractions in order, starting with the smallest.

$\frac{11}{20}$ $\frac{3}{5}$ $\frac{1}{2}$ $\frac{9}{10}$ ____ ____ ____ ____

(4)

21 What is the missing number in this sequence?

25 36 49 ____ 81

22–23 Write the missing numbers in this sequence.

771 767 ____ 759 ____ 751

24 What is the next number in this sequence? 36 49 64 81 ____

(4)

Write **always**, **sometimes** or **never** to make each statement true.

25 Quadrilaterals ____________ have 4 right angles.

26 A triangle ____________ has parallel sides.

27 Cuboids ____________ have 12 edges.

28 A triangular prism ____________ has 6 faces.

(4)

29 What is the area of a square with 5 m sides?

Area = ____________

30 What is the perimeter of a square with 10 cm sides?

Perimeter = ____________

(2)

31–32 Complete this table.

	Length	Width	Area	Perimeter
Rectangle A	4 m	____	20 square metres	18 m
Rectangle B	3 m	____	21 square metres	20 m

2

33 Use a ruler to measure this line. Write your answer in millimetres.

____ mm 1

34 Write the time shown on this clock. ____

35 What time will it be in 45 minutes? ____ 2

36 Write the weight shown on these scales. ____ 1

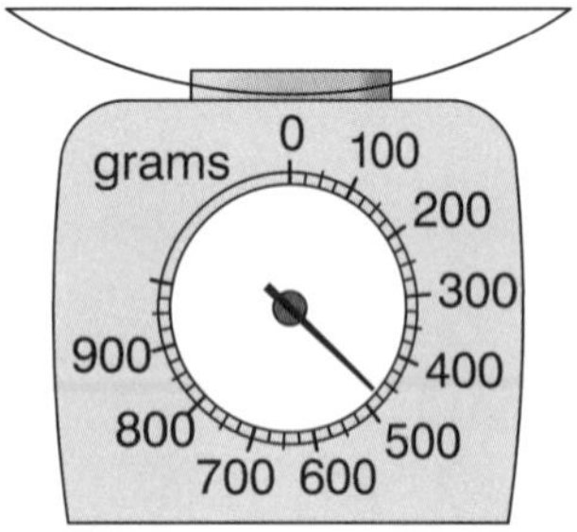

37 Label the arrow pointing W.

38 Label the arrow pointing NE.

39 Label the arrow pointing SW. 3

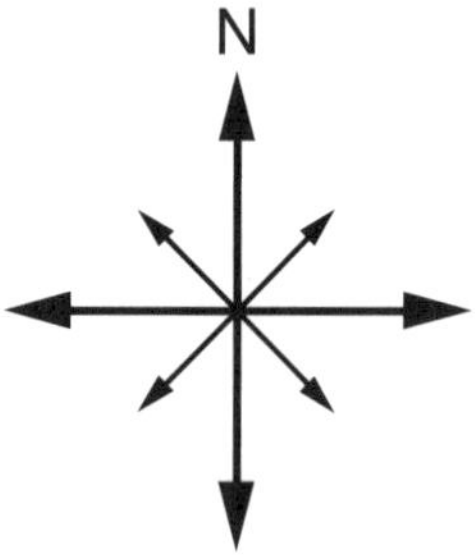

40 Draw a cross at point (0, 7) and label it A.

41 Draw a cross at point (3, 2) and label it B.

42 Draw a cross at point (5, 0) and label it C. 3

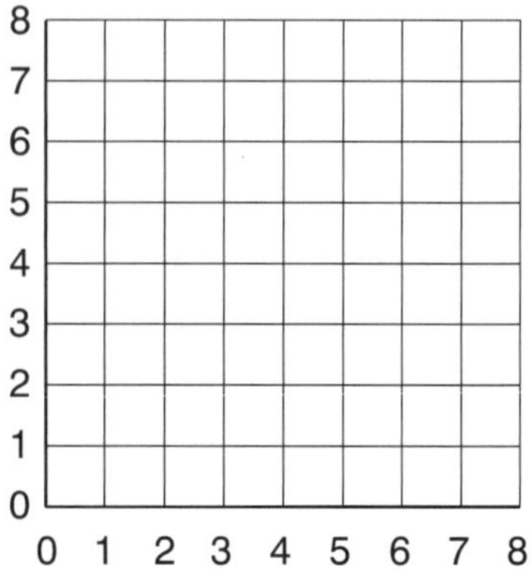

This graph shows the amount of rain for each month.

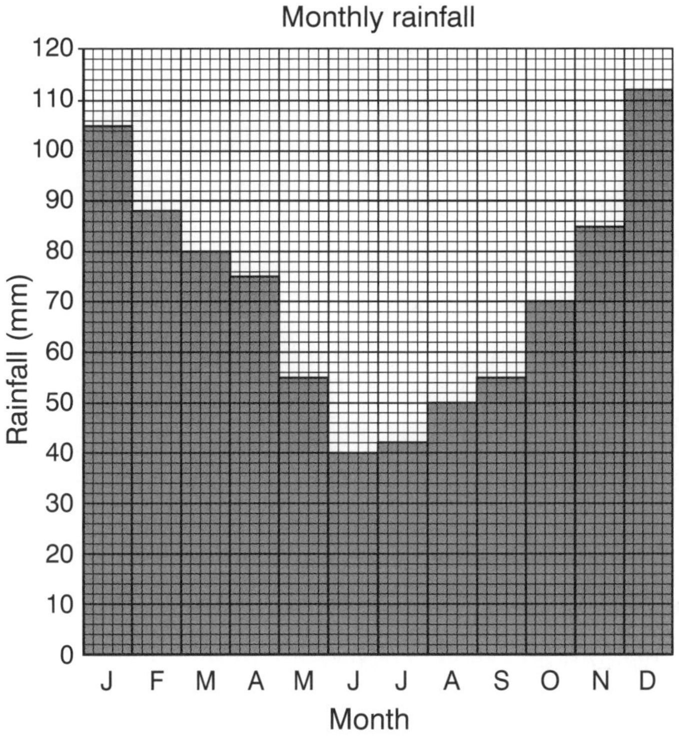

43 Which month had 42 mm of rain? ______________

44 Which month had the same amount of rain as September?

____

45 How much more rain was there in March than June? ______________

46 How many months had more than 60 mm of rain? ______________

4

47–50 Write each circled letter in the correct place on the Venn diagram.

A B C D E F G H I J K L M N O P Q R S T U V W X Y Z

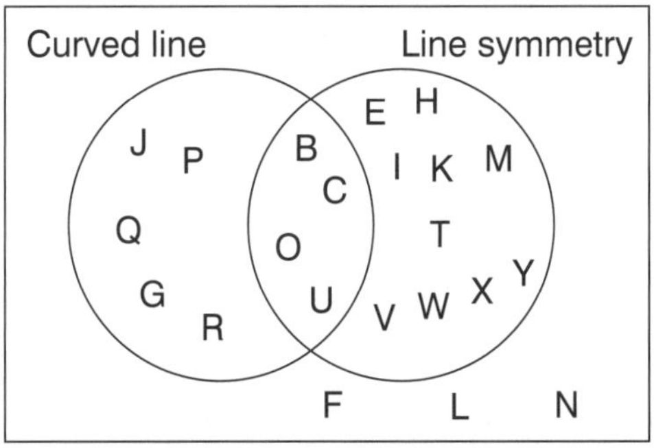

4

Now go to the Progress Chart to record your score! Total 50

Mixed paper 5

Round each of these numbers to the nearest 100.

1 9090 ____ 2 9009 ____

3 9909 ____ 4 9990 ____ 4

Complete these subtractions.

5

$$\begin{array}{r} 7105 \\ -\ \ 976 \\ \hline \\ \hline \end{array}$$

6

$$\begin{array}{r} 8324 \\ -1817 \\ \hline \\ \hline \end{array}$$

2

7 What is 13.7 added to 25.4? ____

8 What is 550 more than 2680? ____

9 What is 14.5 take away 6.4? ____

10 What is 220 less than 2000? ____ 4

11 What is 27 multiplied by 18? ____

Use this grid to help you calculate the answer.

×		
			→ ____
			→ ____

Total: ____ 1

12 Complete this multiplication.

$$\begin{array}{r} 356 \\ \times\ \ \ \ 4 \\ \hline \\ \hline \end{array}$$

13 Complete this division. $6\overline{)2858}$ 2

14 What is the remainder when 73 is divided by 5? ____

15 What is the smallest number that is a multiple of both 4 and 6? ____ 2

16 Circle the number that is a multiple of both 3 and 7.

24 9 42 49 14

17–18 Write the missing factors for 28.

28 → (1, 28) (2, __) (4, __)

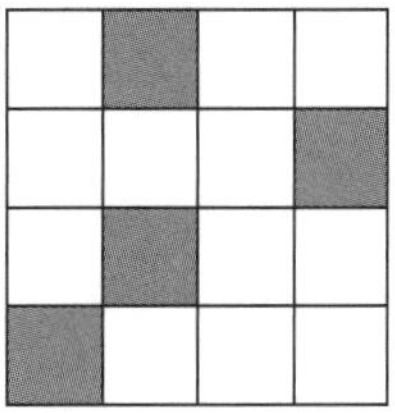

19 What fraction of this shape is shaded? _____

20 Write 20% as a fraction in its lowest form. _____

21 Write $\frac{1}{4}$ as a percentage. _____

22 What is $\frac{1}{8}$ of 24? _____

Look at these number patterns. Write the next two numbers in each pattern.

23–24 16.6 16.1 15.6 _____ _____

25–26 4457 5457 6457 _____ _____

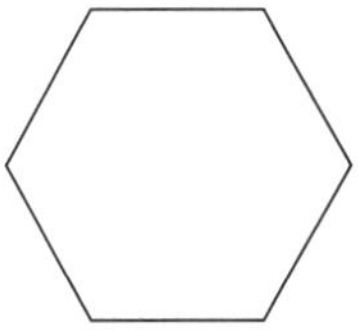

Look at this shape and answer the questions.

27 What is the name of this shape? _______________

28 How many pairs of parallel lines are there in this shape? _____

29 How many right angles are there in this shape? _____

30 How many lines of symmetry does this shape have? _____

31 What is the perimeter of a swimming pool that is 4 m wide and 7 m long? __________

32 What is the area of a book cover that is 20 cm wide by 30 cm long? Underline the correct answer.

50 square centimetres 60 square centimetres

100 square centimetres

500 square centimetres 600 square centimetres

33–34 What are the area and perimeter of this rectangle?

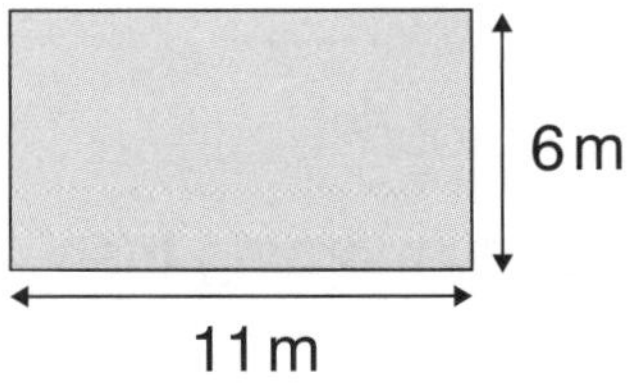

Area = _______________

Perimeter = _______________

35 What is the total weight of these boxes? _____kg _____g

36 The boxes are all the same weight. What is the weight of one box?

____

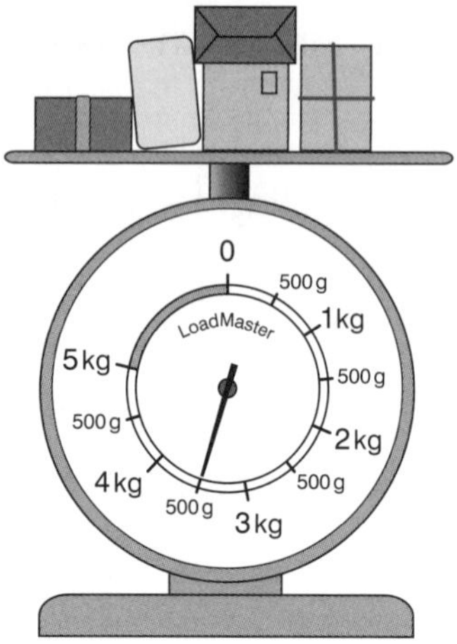

2

37 A cake was put in the oven at 2:55 and took 25 minutes to cook.

At what time was the cake ready to come out of the oven? _____:_____ 1

38 What is 40 mm added to 25 cm? Write the answer in centimetres. _____ 1

39–42 Complete this chart to show where you would be facing after each turn.

Start position, facing:	Turn	End position, now facing:
East	$\frac{1}{4}$ turn anticlockwise	________
North	$\frac{1}{4}$ turn clockwise	________
East	$\frac{1}{2}$ turn clockwise	________
South	$\frac{1}{4}$ turn anticlockwise	________

4

This block graph shows how many birds visited a bird table each morning and afternoon for five days.

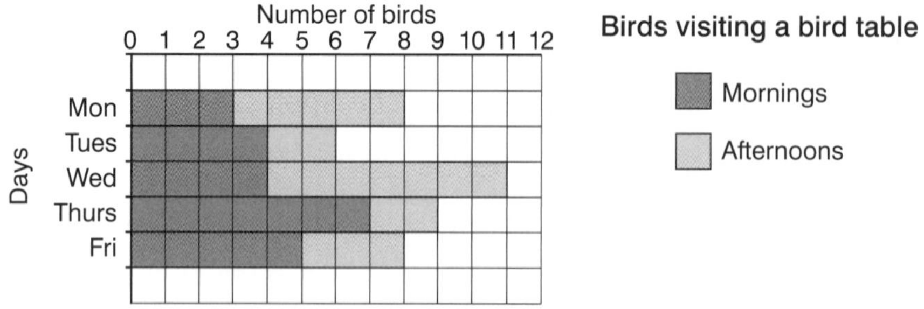

43 How many birds visited the bird table in total on Tuesday? _____

44 How many birds visited the bird table on Monday afternoon? _____

45 How many more birds visited the bird table on Thursday morning than on Thursday afternoon? _____

46 How many birds visited the bird table in total over these five days? ______

4

47–50 Write the letters for each shape A–D in the correct position on the Carroll diagram.

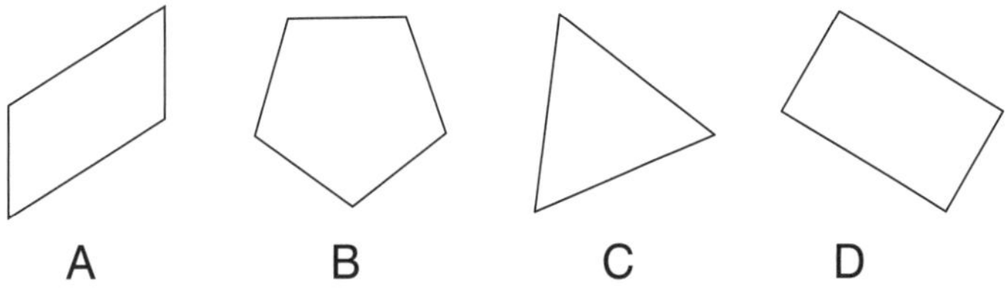

	One or more acute angles	No acute angles
Quadrilateral	______	______
Not a quadrilateral	______	______

4

Now go to the Progress Chart to record your score! Total 50

Mixed paper 6

These are some important dates in the development of communication.

Date	Communication development
1993	'www' was released for public use on the internet
1876	first successful telephone transmission
1929	first regular television broadcasts
1901	first successful transatlantic radio communication

1–4 Write the dates in order, starting with the earliest date.

______ ______ ______ ______

earliest

5 How many years are there between the first successful telephone transmission and the first regular television broadcasts? ______ years

5

6 A fence is put around a playground. Two sides are 25.8 m and the other two sides are 17.4 m.

What is the total length of fence used for the playground? _____ 1

7–9 The digits 3, 4 and 5 are missing. Complete the addition with the digits in the correct place.

$$\begin{array}{r} \square\;4\;7 \\ +\;2\;9\;\square \\ \hline 8\;\square\;0 \\ \hline \end{array}$$

3

10 Which number between 30 and 40 has a remainder of 4 when it is divided by 8? _____ 1

11 A rabbit eats 80 g of food a day.

Would there be enough in a 560 g bag of food to feed the rabbit for a week?

Circle the answer: **yes** **no** 1

12 Multiply 39 by 25. _____

13 Divide 908 by 7. _____ 2

14–17 Write each of these numbers in the correct part of the Venn diagram.

9	**15**	**30**	**54**

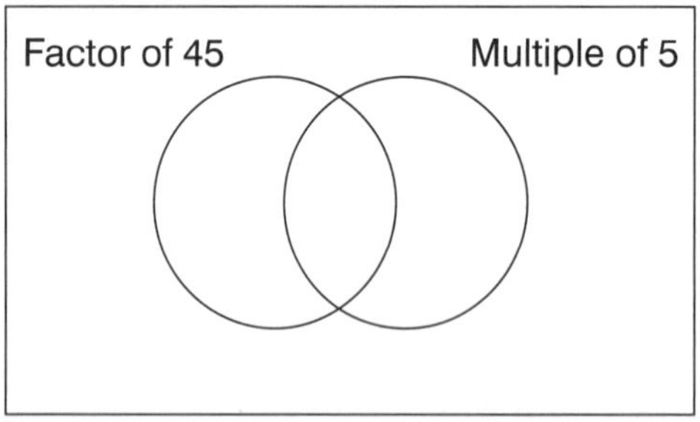

4

18–19 Circle the two fractions that are greater than $\frac{1}{2}$

$\frac{5}{8}$ $\frac{1}{3}$ $\frac{5}{12}$ $\frac{3}{5}$ $\frac{3}{8}$ 2

20 Use two of these digits to make a fraction equal to $\frac{1}{4}$

2	**3**	**4**	**7**	**8**

$\frac{\square}{\square}$ 1

21 Circle the largest number.

$\frac{7}{10}$ 0.25 0.4 $\frac{5}{10}$ 0.75

1

22–23 Write the missing numbers in this sequence.

____ 150 300 600 ____

24 What is the next number in this sequence?

36 25 16 9 ____

25 What is the first number in this sequence?

____ 43 58 73 88 103

4

26–29 Write the letter for each shape in the correct position on the Carroll diagram.

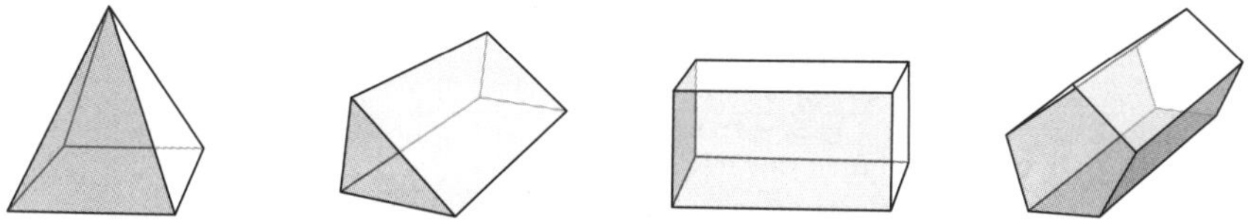

A B C D

	Odd number of vertices	**Even number of vertices**
One or more triangular faces	________	________
No triangular faces	________	________

4

30 What is the perimeter of this shape?

____

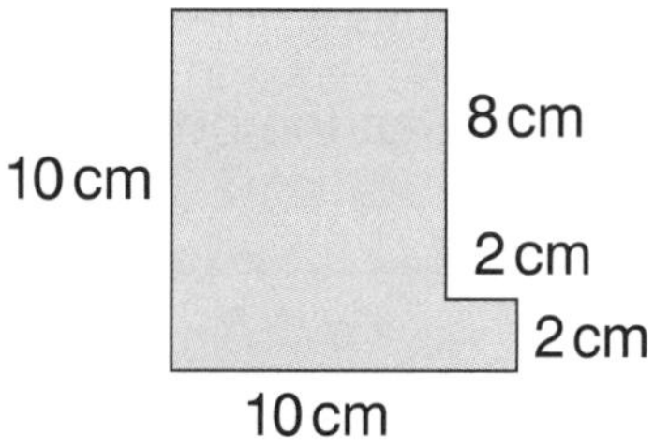

31 What is the area of this shape?
Underline the answer.

100 square centimetres

84 square centimetres

80 square centimetres

2

32 A classroom needs a new carpet. The room is 12 m long and 9 m wide.

What is the area of the classroom? ______________

33 A square has an area of 4 square metres.

Circle the length of the perimeter of this square.

2 m   4 m   6 m   8 m 2

34–35 Circle the smallest quantity. Underline the greatest quantity.

5 ml   6 litres   560 ml   65 ml   50 litres   600 ml 2

36 How many grams are there in two and a half kilograms? _____ g 1

These 6 containers hold 27 litres in total when they are full. Each bottle holds 2 litres.

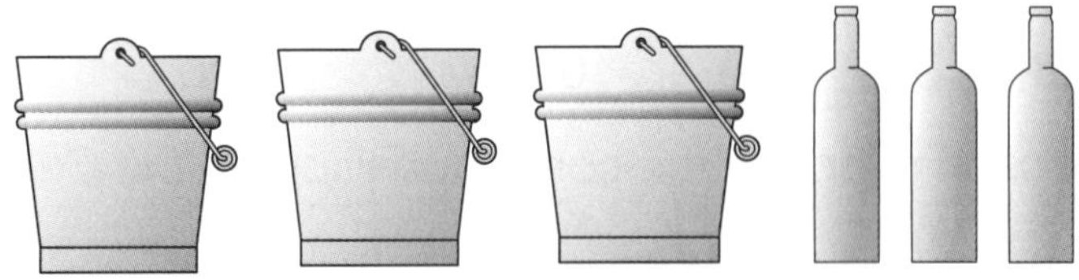

37 How much does each bucket hold? _____ 1

38 Write the coordinates for point A.

(_____ , _____)

39 Draw a cross at point (3, 4) and label it B.

40 If you are standing at point A facing towards point B, are you facing north, south, east or west?

____

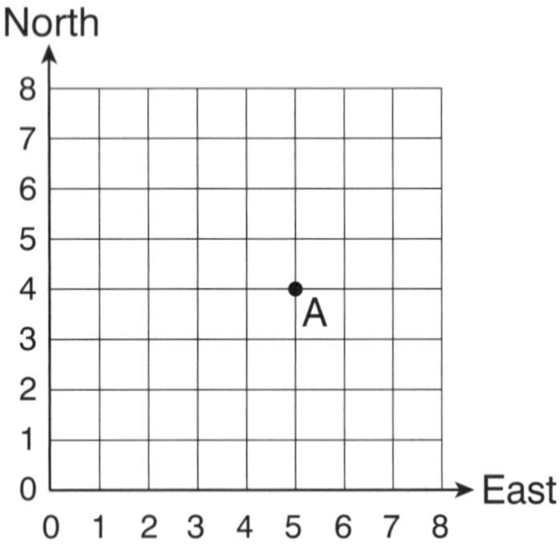

41 Is this statement 'true' or 'false'? Circle the answer.

If you stand at the point (5, 3) and look north, you are facing point A.

true   **false** 4

This graph shows how many children there are in a number of families.

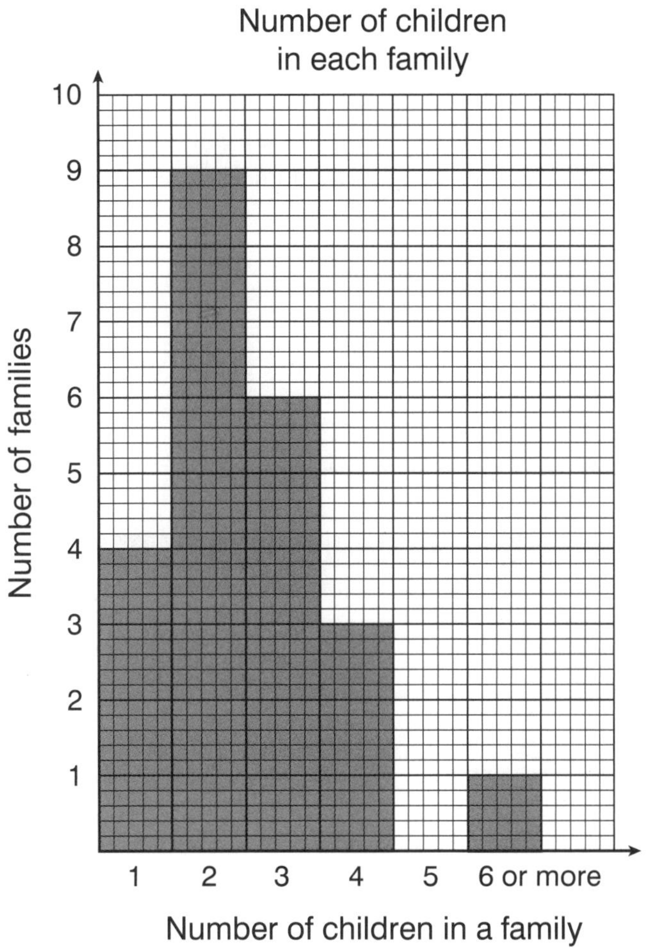

42 How many families have one child? _____

43 There are nine families with the same number of children.

How many children are there in each of these families? _____

44 How many families have four or more children? _____

45 All the families with three children meet for a picnic.

How many children are there in total at the picnic? _____

4

46–49 Write each of the circled numbers in the correct place on the Venn diagram.

~~1~~ ~~2~~ ~~3~~ ~~4~~ ~~5~~ ~~6~~ ~~7~~ ⑧ ~~9~~ ⑩ ~~11~~ ~~12~~ ⑬ ~~14~~ ⑮

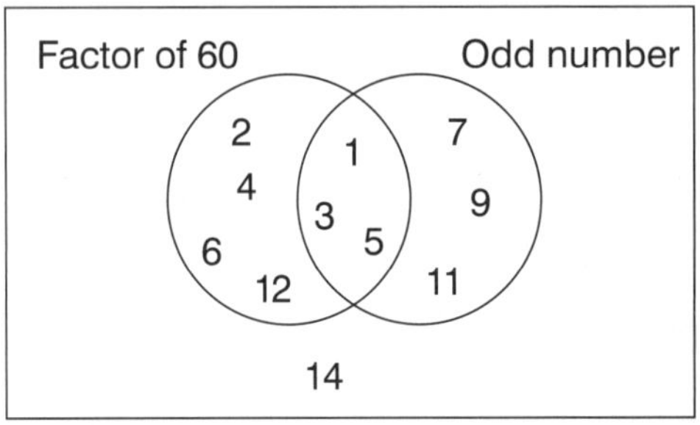

50 Write 30 in the correct section of the Venn diagram.

5

Now go to the Progress Chart to record your score! **Total** **50**